Beyond the Basics:

Unlock Your Dog's Behavior!

First published in 2017 by:

Fenzi Dog Sports Academy Publishing

Copyright © 2017 Denise Fenzi

All uncredited photos © 2017 Denise Fenzi

Designed by: Rebeccah Aube | www.pawsink.com
Paws & Ink! A Creative Blend of Dog Training & Graphic Design

Cover Illustration by: Lili Chin

ISBN NUMBER: 978-0-9887818-9-4

Beyond the Basics
Table of Contents

About the author

Denise Fenzi is a professional dog trainer who specializes in building cooperation and extreme working precision in competitive dog sports teams. Her personal passions are Competitive Obedience and spreading high quality information about no force (motivational) dog training. In addition to travelling worldwide to teach dog training seminars, Denise writes prolifically for the Dog Sports audience, and she also runs a very successful online school for competition dog sports - the Fenzi Dog Sports Academy. You can find all of her books at www.thedogathlete.com, her school at www.fenzidogsportsacademy.com, and her blog at www.denisefenzi.com

Preface
Beyond the Basics

This is a book about dog behavior. Understanding dog behavior. Changing dog behavior. Living in harmony with dog behavior.

This is a book about understanding. Understanding your dog as a living, breathing creature who has emotions, feelings, instincts, a capacity for learning, and rights as a sentient being.

This is a book about training. Training with an eye to creating a warm and mutually satisfying relationship between two species - a human and a dog.

The goal of this book is not to address all of the behavior problems that are typically encountered by dog owners, nor to provide a comprehensive list of all the possible solutions. Instead, this book will help you look at your dog's behavior from a broad perspective; rather than considering your dog's behavior solely in relation to how it affects you, this book will encourage you to consider your dog's behavior and how it affects him. Why does your dog express the behaviors that he does? How have you contributed, either positively or negatively, to the expression of those behaviors? And what options do you have to change those behaviors at a root level rather than simply addressing the symptoms?

When you are finished reading, you will understand why I have made no effort to offer solutions for all the possible problems you might encounter. You will understand that there is no "one-size-fits-all" solution for a problem because each dog is an individual. With your newfound understanding of your dog as an individual, you will be in a good position to begin addressing any current concerns with your dog, or better yet, to prevent problems from developing in the first place.

Of course, this might be a good time to ask a very pointed question: Why do you care? Why do you care if you understand the roots of your dog's behavior problems? Why do you care if your dog is happy about the solutions that you choose? Why do you care if he understands what you are trying to accomplish with your training goals, or if he finds the experience to be stress-free and pleasant?

There are many possible answers. Maybe you care because you like dogs and you want them to be happy. Maybe you care because your philosophy of life is to be gentle with other creatures. Maybe you care because you really want your dog to like you and to develop a positive relationship with you. Or maybe none of this matters to you at all. Maybe you just want your dog to behave in ways that make you happy. That's okay! This book is still for you! In this case, you care because the chances of coming to a successful resolution of problematic dog behavior is much more likely if you address the underlying causes rather than focusing on the symptoms.

Here's a simple example to make this more clear. Let's say that your dog barks excessively when you leave the house. And let's say that in this particular case, the barking is caused by anxiety; your dog's emotional system causes him to feel very anxious and nervous when left alone, so he barks as a symptom of his emotional distress. The barking is upsetting and frustrating for you, so to stop it, you decide to use a shock collar. The idea is simple; if the dog receives a shock at the exact moment he barks, then the dog will associate the barking with the discomfort and will choose to stop barking. And it works! Your dog stops barking!

Unfortunately, because the cause of his barking is mild separation anxiety rather than seeking entertainment, the bark collar has solved your problem (the barking), but not the dog's problem (anxiety). Barking is simply the outwards expression of the emotion, so while the shock collar may stop this specific expression of distress, it doesn't change the fact that the dog is feeling anxious. Indeed, the punishment will make the dog feel a lot worse because now he experiences physical discomfort to go along with his emotional distress.

When strong emotions exist, they require an outlet. So what happens next? Maybe your dog begins to self mutilate when left alone. Now instead of barking and upsetting you and the neighbors, you come home to a dog who is ripping his hair out, chewing his feet bloody, and surrounded by puddles of drool. Or maybe he now eats your furniture and chews your baseboards to bits. And if he's left in a crate during the day, when you open the door, he might climb on you frantically out of extreme relief, further irritating you as he rips at your clothing. You yell at him out of frustration, which causes him to pee on the floor and hide - because now he's afraid of you too.

But he's quiet!

You have jumped from the frying pan to the fire by taking a dog with a mild problem and turning it into a major one... and it could have been easily avoided if the root cause of the dog's barking had been considered before a solution was applied.

And that is why you care about this book, even though it may not tell you how to solve your specific problem. You care because if you can understand your dog's behaviors from his point of view, then the odds that you'll dig a deeper and deeper hole as you try to solve the problem go way down. You'll be able to recognize the hole when you first start digging, and instead of turning it into a first-class grave, you can back out and head in a new direction!

This book is divided into three parts. The first part will consider the reasons dogs behave as they do. These include their basic emotional makeup, physical well-being, quality of training, and temperament. The second part will offer case studies of two problem behaviors - barking and the lack of a recall - with appropriate solutions for specific types of dogs. Take a moment to note that what might be recommended for one dog could be the exact opposite of what is recommended for another. Finally, the third part will offer a plan for evaluating your approach. Did it work? And if it didn't work, why not?

Welcome to the intricate, puzzling, and fascinating world of dog behavior and training. Enjoy the journey!

Part One:
Understanding

The first part of this book will help you develop a very strong understanding of how dogs and their behavior can be the result of things that we do (training), things that we opt not to do (training and management), and things that are inherent to the dog (temperament, emotions, and overall wellness). Each is important to consider when looking at your dog because no one thing alone dictates who your dog is and what he does.

We'll start by considering our dogs' emotions. Although most people acknowledge that their dogs have feelings, few take the time to understand how those feelings impact a dog's ability to learn. By learning about how a dog's behavior might change based on what he is feeling, you can strengthen your relationship with your dog while also making problem behavior less likely.

Next, we'll look at the impact of both physical and mental health on our dogs. It's important to understand some of the common health ailments facing our dogs, and how to determine if a dog is feeling unwell, because these ailments can impact behavior in a variety of ways.

We'll also discuss our dogs' innate temperament, from the typical traits you might expect from your dog to how that might impact your dog's behavior. Learning about what to expect can help you design a training plan to address those potential issues before they even happen!

Finally, we'll spend quite a bit of time discussing training. We'll look at the key components of excellent training, including motivation, how often to reward your dog, and how to set up a training session for success. We'll also discuss the matter of misbehavior, and how you should handle it. All of this will be wrapped up with an entire chapter about how to design a training plan, using one specific (and common!) behavior that many of us struggle with: dogs who jump on other people!

To get the most out of this section, read with an open mind! Some of the information presented here may be unexpected; you might even disagree with it! That's okay. Take the time to really consider whether or not it could apply to your dog before you dismiss it entirely. By analyzing each chapter critically and comparing it to who your dog is, you'll develop a better understanding of what is driving his behavior. In doing so, you'll be able to address problem behaviors by creating a training plan that ultimately makes both of you happier.

Notes

Chapter 1
The Emotional Lives of Dogs

Traditionally, dog trainers have spent little or no energy considering a dog's emotions when training or changing behavior. Trainers or owners who did talk about emotions were often ridiculed and accused of anthropomorphizing (the process of projecting our emotional processes on animals with no consideration for the animal's capacity or the reality of the situation). Instead, dog trainers have focused almost exclusively on how they could change a dog's behavior through the principles of operant conditioning. Training was a quid pro quo equation based on the idea that dogs will maximize their well being. In other words, dogs will do things that benefit them and avoid things that harm them. If a dog's behavior gets him things that he likes, then he will do more of those behaviors. And if a dog's behavior causes things he doesn't like to happen, then he will do less of those behaviors.

That approach makes training sound simple and logical. If you give the dog treats for sitting nicely and push him down when he jumps up, then we should see more sitting. Approached in this manner, it would be simple to list all the random problem behaviors encountered by dog owners and then determine appropriate rewards for good behavior and appropriate punishments for bad behavior. All of the problems will go away and there would be happiness. Right?

Well, no - for two reasons. First of all, operant conditioning assumes a rational participant, and when emotions come into play, reason often goes out the window. And second, strong emotions often cause specific behaviors to happen, not by choice, but as a side effect of the emotion itself. For example, the emotion of fear often makes dogs pace back and forth, or bark, or pant and whine excessively, or jump up on their owners, clinging to them and looking for security. Because pushing them off can exacerbate their feelings of fear and clinginess, this "solution" for jumping can actually make the jumping behavior even more pronounced. Worse, it can stop the jumping, only for it to change to another problematic behavior like submissively urinating. Recognizing that the emotion of fear is driving the behavior of jumping up should dramatically change how we handle the problem behavior.

How Emotions Impact Behavior

When emotions are driving behavior, the dog cannot simply choose to stop doing the behavior without ramifications. The reality is that animals (including people) are quite often NOT rational participants. If that sounds counterintuitive to you and you believe that behavior is largely chosen rather than the result of emotional experiences, perhaps a few examples will help you understand.

The police call and tell you that your son has been in a serious automobile accident and is in the hospital. At that moment, are you in a position to learn new things? Could you choose the behavior of sitting quietly at the table, reading a newspaper while you wait for more information? Would you be able to play a game of chess with your spouse? Of course not! Your fear for your son dominates all rational behavior and overwhelms your capacity for conscious thought. Instead, it's likely that you will pace, or not move at all because you're frozen in fear. You will not be able to listen to conversations that are not about your son because your emotions will not allow it. You may cry (not by choice but as a human expression of fear), you may scream, or you may appear catatonic. But you cannot choose not to be afraid because you do not choose your emotions; you simply experience them, even when you would rather not.

Let's consider a few more emotions.

You discover that your spouse has been having an affair and you're angry beyond reason. Although you had planned to spend the evening catching up on some work that you brought home from the office, there is no chance for that now. Every time you pick up the folders, your mind immediately goes back to the reality of your private life and you drop the papers to return to angry pacing, your fists balled up and your breathing heavy and erratic. You cannot work. You cannot learn. You can barely think, let alone make any decisions or concentrate. You know that if you see your spouse at that moment, you will react badly out of pure rage. You leave the house so you will not be home when he gets there, allowing you to avoid the situation rather than having to show self control that you don't think you can muster. Over time, as you come to accept your spouse's infidelity, you find that your anger is being replaced by a deep sadness that you cannot shake. You find yourself unable to concentrate, to work, or even to do the most basic of life functions like eating and sleeping. You are becoming depressed and once again your emotions are controlling your behavior, very much against your will. You want your rational life back but you can't seem to get there.

The above examples focus on unhappy emotions like fear, rage, and sadness. So maybe negative emotions can severely impact learning and our choice of behaviors, but how about happy emotions? Could those possibly impact our outward expression of our behavior? Yes, they can.

Let's say you just won the lottery - 10 million dollars! You are excited! Beside yourself with joy! You cannot wait to tell all your friends! But first, you'll need to complete some paperwork and answer some questions. What is your social security number? How much did you claim on last year's tax return? Do you want to take the money as a lump sum or over twenty years? You find yourself struggling to participate in this very important interview. Heck, you can barely remember your own name, let alone your social security number or the definition of an annuity. Fortunately, the lottery secretary has seen this before, so she gives you lots of time to calm down; indeed, she suggests that you go get a friend to help you because she's pretty sure you'll get almost everything wrong if you try to do the interview alone. So while your friend writes down a list of required documents and decisions to be made, you run around the house, occasionally letting out screams of excitement and leaping around, looking a lot like a three-year-old on Christmas morning. You may be experiencing a wonderful emotion for a wonderful reason, but you're not functioning well because strong emotions block rational thought.

Now let's consider our dogs.

A large and aggressive dog lunges towards your dog at dog training school. Your dog is not physically injured, but he is absolutely terrified by the encounter. He can't stop looking where the dog had been standing. Even though he had been doing fine in his training up until this point, now he simply stands catatonic in the middle of the room. He is not in a position to learn because he does not feel safe. More so, he cannot simply choose to feel better any more than you can, even when he realizes that the other dog is no longer present. From the handler's point of view, the threat is gone, so the handler may well expect the dog to get on with his training. But in the same way that a human who is almost attacked on the street cannot simply move on after the police come and arrest the person, your dog cannot simply move on either. His emotions must be processed before rational thought can take over again. How long that takes is a function of the animal experiencing them, not the desires of the owner.

How about a happy emotion like joy? Does that emotion also block rational thought when our dogs experience it? Yes.

Your dog was just reunited with you after two weeks in a boarding kennel. He is overjoyed to see you again and can't stop jumping up on you with happiness! In fact, he is so excited that he can't see how irritated you are becoming about his muddy pawprints on your clothes. Now you're both under the influence of emotions: your dog is happy to be reunited with you, and you're frustrated because your clothes are getting dirty. At that moment, it's likely that neither one of you is going to make very good decisions.

Emotions don't always prevent a dog from learning. Sometimes, your dog's emotions may actually set him up for a great learning situation. For example, let's say that your dog is left alone all day long with nothing to do. He is bored and desperately looking for something to do, so he starts to dig the dirt out of your houseplants. Later, he teaches himself how to climb up your pantry shelves to where you keep the dog biscuits. He IS in a position to learn - in fact, learning solves the feeling of boredom - but you're not there to teach him something useful. So instead, he learns about wrecking your house and stealing dog biscuits. In this case, the feeling of boredom, and your dog's desire to eliminate that feeling, leads to problematic learning.

In all of these examples, both human and canine, how the individual is feeling is the driving force behind the expressed behavior. Since we do not choose what we feel at any given time, we're stuck with our emotions, whether we like them or not! And since strong emotions cause behavior to happen - whether we like those behaviors or not - we're stuck with them, too. If you choose to ignore the emotions and focus solely on the behaviors, you're likely to get nowhere in your attempts to create change. Worse yet, you might actually exacerbate the problem.

The fearful dog may try to run away and refuse to come back, irritating the owner who knows that the aggressive dog left the dog school an hour ago. The excited, happy-to-see-you dog can't settle down! And the bored dog is wrecking your house. In all of these examples, the solution lies in addressing the emotion, not the behavior. Solve the emotion and you solve the behavior.

When an animal is in a state of emotional overload, we say that the dog is "over threshold." The dog's emotions are so great that the dog can no longer function effectively. In short, the dog cannot learn very well at that time. When a dog is over threshold, operant conditioning works very poorly because the dog is not rational at all. Only when a dog is "under threshold" is he capable of conscious thought, and only then can training take hold.

Adults, Pre-Verbal Children, and Dogs

In the above human examples of strong emotion, we discussed adults who have learned how to moderate their emotions, accept the realities of day-to-day existence, and find ways to cooperate even when they don't want to. Because of this experience, adults are not likely to be completely overwhelmed with emotion very often. So how do these examples change when we talk about a two-year-old child instead?

As every parent knows, toddlers experience (and express) emotions intensely and frequently. Everything is new and overwhelming to the toddler, and as a result, they have neither the developmental capacity nor the motivation to modify their emotional expression. Toddlers are routinely supervised because we know that under the influence of strong emotions, they will make really bad decisions like running out into the street after a ball, lashing out and hitting people, or grabbing attractive but dangerous items. In fact, we manage their behavior by holding their hands when we are walking on a busy street, or we avoid the situation altogether until the child is older and more able to stay reliably "under threshold."

And your dog? Well, research into the cognitive capabilities of dogs shows that dogs are roughly equivalent to a two-year-old child. You can assume that your dog's capacity for controlling his behavior is on par with that of a toddler.

Yes, your dog can be trained to perform specific behaviors (come when called, stay, wait at the door, toilet outside). And yes, your dog can also learn not to perform other behaviors (digging in your garden, barking in his crate, pulling on leash). However, you'll find that this training goes a lot better when the dog is not under the influence of overwhelming emotions that block effective learning. And, like with a two-year-old child, there is also a place for recognizing when your expectations are not reasonable, making management the most logical solution. This is why we leash our dogs instead of relying on training when we walk them near busy roads.

The Ideal Emotional State for Learning

Does this mean we want to work with dogs who are devoid of emotion, staring vacantly into space? Absolutely not! We want to train a dog who is engaged with us! We want to train a dog who is happy, alert, focused, and motivated by whatever rewards we might have to offer. Dogs, like people, are curious and want to learn! We want a dog who is emotionally ready, willing, and able to learn!

When You Ignore Your Dog's Emotions

There are two significant effects of ignoring a dog's emotional state. First, if the problem behavior is a direct result of the emotional state, then attempting to address the behavior directly without addressing the underlying emotion will create new problems. For example, if your dog is afraid to go for a walk because of the dogs who lunge and bark at him from behind their fences, you could attach the leash before you leave the house so that he has no choice but to come along. Now what happens? Well, after a few days, you may find that when you call him to attach the leash, he's nowhere to be found. Now you have two problems: a dog who is afraid to be walked, and a dog who will not come when called. If you persist, trap him in the corner, attach the leash, and pull him out the door, then what? The next time you trap him in the corner and reach for his collar, he may well pee on your floor or snap at your hand. Now you're up to three problems. How many problems do you plan to create before you simply accept that your dog is fearful on his walk and address the root emotional problem?

The second significant effect of ignoring your dog's emotional state is that you'll find that training is slower and more laborious than it needs to be. Dogs who are comfortable, engaged, and not under the influence of significant emotions learn very quickly because they can concentrate on what you are doing together. Dogs who are fearful, overly excited, angry, or experiencing any other overwhelming emotions do not retain information well because they can't concentrate on learning. A simple recall cue that would take a confident and engaged dog two days to learn now takes two weeks, creating a lot of frustration for both the dog and the handler, and eroding the pleasure that you both should experience during training.

What is My Dog Feeling?

How can we know what dogs are feeling? Obviously we cannot ask them, and since they have different body shapes, vocalizations, and expressions than humans, it's not always obvious what might be taking place inside those furry little heads. Now what? We have two basic strategies. First, we can become keen observers of dog body language and behavior. Second, we can ask ourselves this question: "If a two-year-old were showing this behavior under similar circumstances, what emotions might I suspect were at play?" Let's look at each of these in turn.

Dog Body Language

Dog body language can be quite difficult to read, so it's important to consider the context when interpreting behavior. Not only do you need to consider the environment (for example, dogs will pant when they're hot, but also when they're stressed), you also need to look at all of the body parts together. Although many people attempt to correlate each type of movement with a specific emotion, the easier approach is simply to compare the overall picture of a distressed dog to a happy dog.

What does a distressed dog look like? Generally speaking, you'll probably see a dog who pants when he's not hot, avoids eye contact, keeps his head or body low, yawns when he's not tired, licks his lips in the absence of food, shows the whites of his eyes, has large dilated pupils, tucks his tail between his legs, or holds it straight up and very stiff. Keep in mind that all stress signals also have a normal variant; a dog may lick his lips because he is stressed, but he may also lick his lips if he has just finished a meal! There is no reason to assume stress unless the context suggests it!

You can tell that your dog is becoming overwhelmed with stress if he freezes, runs away, or begins to fight back. All of these options are possible depending on the situation or the individual dog. Some dogs respond to stress by becoming passive and quiet, with extreme stress causing a dog to literally freeze and stop moving. Anxious dogs will attempt to cling to their owners for support. Other dogs become frantic, excited, or start running around for no apparent reason at all. These dogs might rely on themselves to feel safe, scanning the environment obsessively and showing an inability to relax and settle. Some especially fearful dogs will try to drive away something that they perceive as dangerous by barking or lunging. It doesn't matter if it truly is dangerous or not. If your dog thinks it is, you need to take it seriously.

Do not attempt to make your dog "face his fears." Minimizing and ignoring fear issues does not make them go away. When you either ignore fear or force your dog to face it in an effort to "prove" that something is not dangerous, you are heading down the wrong path. You can easily end up with total shut down or with defensive aggression.

Here's a human example to make this more clear. Let's say you're afraid of mice. In an effort to help you adapt, your best friend "helpfully" locks you in a room with mice everywhere, crawling all over you. Maybe you start screaming. Maybe you lash out, trying to stomp on the mice. Maybe you become so overwhelmed with fear that you become catatonic. Regardless of how you react, how do you think you would feel about the friend who put you in that situation? Would you trust her or want to spend time with her again? Probably not. Your dog is the same way. Don't become the enemy.

Fearful behavior needs to be taken seriously and worked through thoughtfully and carefully. It can take hundreds, maybe even thousands, of pleasant and positive events to overcome the effects of one negative event. If you think your dog has more than a mild problem with fear, you need to contact a dog training behaviorist to help you. Learning from a book is fine for most training and for mild behavior problems, but if you're dealing with more extreme behavior, you need professional help to guide you.

How about anger? Dogs experience anger for many of the same reasons that people do, usually because they have lost something they want, like food, toys, or attention. Rather than walking away and accepting that loss, they will try to get it back with threats. You might see your dog growling, posturing stiffly, making hard eye contact, or - if all else fails - lunging, snapping, and even biting! Although most dog bites occur out of fear, the reality is that dogs can become angry and react badly as a result. In the same way that very fearful dogs require specialized professional help, if your dog is showing strong aggression and a willingness to use physical force to "get his way," then you need professional help, not a book. Contact a dog behaviorist to help you.

So what do happy dogs look like? Happy dogs have open and relaxed body language. They tend to approach somewhat sideways, wiggling all over! Their tails wag fast and loose. Their eyes are open and bright, their ears are forward and up or very relaxed, and their focus tends to shift easily from one interesting option to another. If you're not sure how this looks, pay attention to your dog's behavior when you come home after a brief absence and he's cheerfully following you through the house. Keep in mind that even happy emotions can be overwhelming, which might tinge your dog's behavior with a frantic quality. For example, in that first minute after you get home, your dog might be happy to see you, but he might also be jumping on you, vocalizing, panting heavily, and showing wide eyes and dilated pupils. Or, he might simply run around, releasing his happy/frantic energy with movement. Or, his focus may be scattered: leaping on you, and then running off to grab a toy, and then back to you!

Happy body language is always good but - and this is big - remember that if the dog is <u>overwhelmed</u> by his emotions, he will not be receptive to training until he is in a calmer state of mind. A "too happy and excited" dog is just as much at risk of showing problematic behavior as a "too scared or unhappy" dog.

One of the most useful indicators of happy or distressed body language is a solid understanding of what your dog normally looks like under a variety of circumstances. If you know what your dog looks like when you're engaged in your dog's favorite activity - like playing ball - then you know what one variant of happy looks like. If you have seen your dog when he was startled by a stranger on the street, then you know what fearful body language looks like. All of this requires that you pay attention; take the time to observe your dog in your day to day life and you'll be well ahead of the game.

If Your Dog Was a Toddler

The second way to interpret your dog's behavior is to imagine that he is a toddler. This requires combining what you see in the dog's behavior with what you know of the context and then making some educated guesses.

Let's say your dog is acting hyper. He has just been released from his crate after a long night's sleep. He's moving around a lot, chewing your things, and maybe even mouthing you too! He's grabbing your shoes and running off with them. If this was a toddler, what would you be thinking? Probably that he's bored. So what's the solution? Do something!

Now how about this. Your dog is acting hyper, but he's been out all day, visiting people, playing ball at the park, and socializing with other dogs. He's had dinner and now you want to watch TV but he can't stop moving. He's chewing on things, maybe even mouthing you, too! He's grabbing your shoes and running off with them. If this was a toddler, what would you be thinking? That he's tired! He's had a busy day and now he needs to sleep. So what's the solution? Put him to bed! He may complain in the crate for a couple of minutes, but if the issue really is exhaustion, he will soon fall asleep.

If all you look at is behavior and emotion without context, then it's very likely that you'll head down the wrong path. In one case, you have a bored dog, and in the other you have a tired dog - both are creating the same problematic behavior but the appropriate solution requires knowledge of the context. If you ask yourself what the problem would be if your dog was a toddler, you may well find the solution as a result.

Guessing Wrong

In truth, we cannot know what a pre-verbal child or baby is thinking, but that doesn't mean that we don't try to understand what he needs! When your baby is crying, you try to find the most likely cause. Sometimes you'll be right; you'll be able to solve the problem and the crying will stop. Other times you'll be wrong and you'll have to try something else. It's okay to be wrong; just keep looking for the answer! Humans as a species spend an enormous amount of time refining our social skills with each other, trying to understand the emotions and behaviors of others so that we can get along most effectively in the world. If you take this approach with your dog, you'll reap enormous benefits.

Of course, sometimes you'll set yourself up to guess wrong. Let's say you just came home from a movie to find that your dog has peed on your bed, ripped up your favorite book, barked for an hour straight, and is now sound asleep in a happy puddle in the middle of the couch. You decide to look at this from a human point of view. Why would you pee on your best friend's bed, scream nonstop, and rip up her stuff? You think for a moment and conclude that your dog must be angry because you went out and had fun without him! He made a big mess for you to find when you came home in order to punish you before falling asleep, smugly dreaming about how he taught you a lesson.

And herein lies the danger with anthropomorphism.

You didn't look at the situation from the viewpoint of an emotional two-year-old; you looked at it as an older child or as an adult! You attached YOUR emotions, your anger at the destruction, to what you found when you got home. You assumed an emotion like spite, yet there is no evidence that dogs have anything like that. You gave him the emotions of an adult human, and he is far from that!

Dogs (and toddlers) are not thinking about what happened earlier - they are thinking about what is happening right now! They live in the moment. Dogs are not thinking about how you'll feel when you come home and find the mess; they are simply reacting to whatever is happening right now, and whatever emotions come along with those events. Dogs do not think about what you did yesterday unless something you are doing right now reminds them of it (like when you're getting the leash to take them for a walk in the neighborhood and yesterday that walk was scary).

Dogs do not plot revenge or try to figure out how to make you suffer. That's a very complex thing to do! While there is very compelling evidence that dogs experience basic emotions like anger and joy, there is no scientific evidence that dogs feel more complex emotions like guilt or spite. While your dog might suffer if and when you punish him, it does not cause him to feel remorse over what has already happened.

So if you assume that your dog is acting with the intention of creating discomfort for you, then you are giving your dog credit for significantly more emotional abilities than he possesses. Dogs do not experience those emotions. Neither do two-year-olds. It's a bad trap to start assuming that your dog is out to get you. Remember, when you're trying to use human motivations to guess what motivated a dog, use the motivations of a two-year-old. If you're not familiar with two-year-olds, ditch that strategy entirely! Instead, just consider your dog as a creature who lives in the moment, with whatever is happening at that time.

Summary

This chapter has focused on the relationships between emotion and behavior. The important things to keep in mind are that dogs experience a range of emotions in much the same way as a two-year-old does, and that the impact of those emotions can be responsible for problematic behavior while also preventing you from creating any meaningful change. Consider your dog's behavior and body language within the context of the circumstances before you try to solve a problem. If you understand your dog's emotions, you're much more likely to be successful at creating a training plan that works, and odds are pretty good that your dog will have a lot more fun with you, too!

Chapter 2
Pain, Illness, and Behavior

© Stephanie Colman

When we acquire a dog to share our lives with, we immediately assume we have a physically and mentally sound animal. We assume that we will live with that animal in relative good health for a very long time, right into doggy old age, and we set our expectations accordingly. Unfortunately, sometimes what we get is different. Dogs, like people, are all over the map in terms of overall health and a likelihood to suffer from chronic medical conditions or undiagnosed pain. And dogs, like people, will experience pain and illness differently, depending on what they are doing at any given time.

Because physical and mental discomfort can have an enormous impact on a dog's behavior, it behooves us to look for signs of pain or illness whenever we are facing behavioral challenges in our pets. So what are the medical issues that dogs suffer from, and how might they affect observable behavior? How can we tell if our dogs are feeling well? If the vet says a dog is healthy, can we rely on that? How significant are mental disorders in dogs, and what types of symptoms might we see if our dog is suffering from mental illness?

The purpose of this chapter is not to provide a comprehensive list of physical and mental disorders that can cause pain and suffering. Instead, in the same way that it's important to understand how the emotions our dogs experience both cause and exacerbate behavior problems, it is also important to be aware how the physical sensations of illness and pain can directly and indirectly influence how our dogs behave. This chapter will explore the link between physical or mental issues and behavior problems so that they can be either addressed or ruled out before developing a training plan.

Common Health Issues in Puppies and Adolescent Dogs

While significant health concerns become more likely with age, there are a wide range of illnesses and painful conditions that are not uncommon in puppies and young dogs. Let's look at a few of these.

Teething is painful for pups and babies alike. When puppies are getting adult teeth to replace their baby ones, it is common to see a lot of chewing. If puppies don't have things to chew on to relieve their discomfort, then they may look for things to chew on, quite possibly at the expense of your house and personal possessions. Because dogs develop habits at this age about what is acceptable to chew on and what is not, it is very important that you make sure they develop the habits that you want to see in adulthood!

Stomach problems are common with young puppies, especially as new foods are introduced or due to intestinal parasites. Both can cause problems with diarrhea, which can severely complicate housebreaking. Pay attention to the possibility of stomach upset when your puppy is struggling to toilet appropriately!

"Growing pains" (also called panosteitis) and joint/bone problems can cause chronic and significant pain in dogs. Some dogs show clear signs of distress such as limping, but other dogs hide their pain most of the time. Only a keen observer will notice the more subtle signs of pain. Regardless, the effect of chronic pain can strongly influence the dog's behavior and should be considered as a possible cause of problematic behavior, particularly in the larger or faster growing breeds of dogs.

Allergies can cause non-stop misery for some dogs. These unfortunate animals scratch obsessively, bite at their bodies, or suffer from intestinal distress. All of this disrupts their normal life activities and causes sleep deprivation. This, in turn, lowers their overall tolerance and creates additional behavior issues.

Thyroid problems are well known to cause a wide range of behavior issues in dogs, from mental disorders to aggression to apathetic behavior. Fortunately, thyroid issues are relatively easy to treat once they are diagnosed.

Eye and ear infections, dental problems, skin disorders, yeast infections... the list goes on and on. And of course, there are the forms of pain that humans know are real, but that have neither an obvious cause nor a direct solution. Severe headaches, muscle aches, painful joints, nerve pain, neck pain - all of these cause very real pain, yet without sophisticated diagnostic tools, they are unlikely to be detected in dogs.

All of these medical problems are common, cause chronic suffering, and may continue undiagnosed for significant periods of time. Since our dogs cannot tell us what their bodies are feeling, we have to rely on subtle behavior changes to let us know that something isn't quite right, even as we struggle to figure out what the problem actually is.

Symptoms of Physical Pain

Dogs in distress tend to show both physical and behavioral changes. These changes can be quite subtle, and the owner may need to do a little detective work to determine if there is a medical problem that needs to be addressed. Some classic signs of pain in dogs include panting excessively, shivering, drooling, and excessive drinking. Even if your dog has only occasional episodes, there is an issue that needs to be investigated.

One of the biggest clues that something is not quite right is simply a change from normal. For example, let's say your housebroken dog starts to have accidents in the house. Toilet training accidents can be a clue that your dog may have bladder stones, a hormone imbalance that needs to be addressed, stomach issues, or an anxiety disorder. Or maybe your dog who has always finished every meal begins to occasionally refuse meals, or your gulper begins to eat slowly and carefully, as if chewing or swallowing is no longer comfortable. Anything from dental problems to intestinal upset to something quite serious indeed could be the culprit. What if your dog who has always slept happily on the floor starts seeking out your furniture or beds? He might be looking for softer surfaces because something hurts.

You should also be on the lookout for changes to your dog's usual temperament and personality. Concerning behavior changes might include loss of tolerance for other family members, startling easily, snapping, overreacting to situations that used to be well tolerated, hiding from or avoiding family members, unusual aggression with no apparent cause, or a lack of enthusiasm for activities that used to be enjoyed.

Dogs are notorious for hiding pain until it becomes rather extreme. While very occasional signs of discomfort in an otherwise happy and healthy dog might deserve a "wait and see" attitude, strong signs of pain such as yelping or actively protecting body parts indicate great discomfort that requires a trip to a veterinarian.

Mental Pain (Mental Illness)

It is well understood that humans and dogs share a variety of mental illnesses, including phobias, PTSD, compulsive disorders, separation anxiety, generalized anxiety, depression, and dementia. Unfortunately, the stigma of mental illness that surrounds humans and prevents them from getting much-needed help has created an equivalent stigma around our pets, preventing us from recognizing and addressing canine mental health issues that would benefit greatly from behavior training and medication. The fact is, mental suffering can cause extreme pain. In many cases, the same medications that have been found to provide relief for humans also provide relief for our animals, which strongly suggests that the experience of mental suffering is similar for humans and dogs alike.

Age of onset varies, but mental disorders often begin or progress around adolescence, just when people are expecting their dogs to get easier! Here are some examples of widely recognized mental illness and pain-inducing mental disorders in dogs.

Dogs experiencing separation anxiety are actively distressed when left. They may be unable to eat when alone, vocalize continuously, drool excessively, or destroy items. In some cases, they have full-blown panic attacks and chew or scratch at doors, floors, and walls. If your dog's behavior leaves you unable to lead a normal life due to his extreme behavior, then you are likely dealing with separation anxiety.

Dogs who have compulsive behaviors engage in obsessive, repetitive behaviors, and appear unable to stop. At first glance, it may seem the dog enjoys the activity. For example, a dog might obsessively chase shadows in the back yard until he falls over in exhaustion, only to get up and start again. But on closer inspection, you'll notice that the dog is actually distressed, possibly whining, pacing, or panting. While dogs with compulsive behaviors may be temporarily distracted, they will return to the activity as soon as the stimulus reappears, even something as simple as a breeze causing a tree leaf to move, creating a shadow.

Other examples of compulsive behavior include spinning, pacing, chewing on body parts, licking people or objects like walls, digging at the floor, or bothering other animals in the house intensely and obsessively. If they are blocked from engaging in one obsessive behavior, it is common for the dog to develop a new compulsive behavior, like hunting imaginary insects or chewing the base of the tail.

It's important to recognize that dogs expressing compulsive behaviors do not enjoy these activities. They are compelled to engage in those activities, even if the behavior causes them pain, distress, or exhaustion. Just as a human with compulsive behaviors cannot simply choose to stop, neither can your dog. Whenever the dog's behavior becomes so significant that you believe the activity is causing either physical or mental discomfort, consider consulting a veterinary behaviorist for help.

Generalized anxiety disorder is also quite common in dogs and expresses itself as fear without an obvious cause. These dogs tend to pant excessively, show dilated pupils and signs of physical agitation, pace, appear unable to relax, continually scan the environment (called hypervigilance), and have problems with inter-dog aggression within their homes. These dogs also frequently suffer from stomach disorders which lead to chronic diarrhea or vomiting. In short, they're chronically anxious, which prevents them from enjoying their lives much at all.

Dogs can also suffer from depression as a result of a chemical imbalance in the brain or a poor living environment, much the same as people. Dogs who struggle with depression may start out as perfectly normal puppies, but over time, they seem to shut down and no longer enjoy normal life activities like eating, going for walks, or training with their human partners. They may also show disturbed sleep cycles. When your dog gets to the point where you start to wonder where your happy dog has gone, and if your vet cannot find physical causes for your dog's distress, it's time to consider whether depression might be causing the problem. Medication exists that can help your dog and may be the key to getting your happy dog back.

Identifying Mental Distress

The most obvious indications that an animal is suffering from mental illness are often quite similar for both people and dogs. A dog or person with a phobia will strongly avoid or even panic when they believe they will encounter the thing they are phobic of. A dog with anxiety will begin to whine, pace, pant heavily, and possibly claw at his owner in an outward expression of panic and dread. Dogs with dementia appear unable to recognize their own homes, familiar animals or caregivers, and are often erratic and irrational in their behavior.

Most mental illness in dogs is related to the emotion of fear. For whatever reason - often a genetic predisposition, unfortunate experience, or a combination of both - the dog has a strong fear response to experiences that other dogs tolerate well or are able to recover from. Rather than recovering and becoming more resilient over time, dogs with fear-based mental illness tend to become more and more agitated the more often they encounter the stress-inducing stimulus. For example, a dog with separation anxiety may first become anxious and agitated when crated. Soon he becomes anxious when the owner approaches the dog near the crate. Then it's when the dog realizes the owner is getting ready to leave the house. Eventually, it can progress to the point that the dog lives in a state of chronic agitation.

Let's be clear that mental pain can cause extreme suffering. It cannot be dismissed simply because it's not physical in nature. In humans, mental illness is a leading cause of suicide; that alone should make it clear that the pain from mental suffering is quite severe. There's really no excuse for allowing animals we are responsible for to suffer intensely when we have medications that can improve their quality of life. In the same way that you would not withhold medication from a dog who is crying in physical pain, there is also no reason to withhold medication from a dog who is expressing significant emotional distress - nor to see it as a last resort.

Finding Undiagnosed Illness or Pain

It is common for dogs to live with serious illness for months or even years without the owner knowing about it. It isn't until the dog's condition deteriorates that the illness becomes obvious. Serious illnesses such as brain tumors, cancer, and kidney stones can exhibit like this, causing the dog pain for extended periods of time without the owner's awareness, often with problematic behavior being the only symptom of the underlying physical problem.

It is also relatively common for an owner to come to the conclusion that something is wrong, even though trips to the vet do not provide a definitive diagnosis. Maybe the symptoms come and go, making it very difficult for a veterinarian to identify a cause, or maybe the symptoms are so vague and common that it's almost impossible to pin it down to a specific cause.

If a trip to your regular veterinarian does not provide answers, consider contacting the place where you got the dog. If your dog's issues are genetic, you may discover that parents, siblings, or other close relatives have a medical condition that will shed light on your dog's issues.

In some cases, it's worth talking to your veterinarian about giving your dog a trial of pain medication. If your dog's physical or behavioral symptoms abate, then you know that the dog is experiencing pain, even if you don't know the source of that pain. You can then talk to your vet about the options, which may range from doing absolutely nothing, to keeping the dog on pain medication without a diagnosis, to performing a series of invasive or specialized tests. Only you and your veterinarian can make those decisions for your dog's specific situation.

Do Not Assume...

We cannot assume that a dog is not in pain just because he is not vocalizing his distress or showing other obvious signs. Unlike people, dogs rarely express their pain openly.

We cannot assume that simply because a dog is young that he must be healthy. Undiagnosed illness and pain is quite common across the age spectrum.

We cannot assume that a dog's willingness to engage in beloved activities like playing ball or eating dinner means the dog is not suffering from pain or sickness. Just like a very sick child might insist that she is well enough to go to her best friend's birthday party, a dog might mask pain or sickness for a chance to play ball in the local park.

We cannot assume that dogs who show signs of mental disorders were abused or are somehow being mistreated, nor can we assume that lack of prior trauma rules out mental illness.

We cannot assume that getting an "all clear" from the vet means the dog is not experiencing pain. A wide variety of painful problems like headaches, nerve pain, and mental illness are not easily diagnosed on a routine visit to the vet. If the dog's behavior suggests that something is wrong, honor that information.

The Effects of Undiagnosed or Ignored Pain and Illness

Both veterinarians and pediatricians struggle with the challenge of nonverbal patients who have no ability to communicate where the pain is, what it feels like, and other pertinent information that might allow a medical professional to make an accurate diagnosis and treatment plan. Since pain tends to have a universal and deleterious effect on both human and canine behavior, it's important to consider what happens if pain continues without being addressed.

Dogs experiencing pain or illness may exhibit behavior problems that are a direct result of the illness. For example, aggression may directly result from a brain tumor, urinating in the house might be the result of bladder stones, and refusing to sit on cue could be the result of a painful joint disorder.

Dogs experiencing pain or illness may also exhibit behavior problems as an indirect result of the illness. In the same way that humans in pain are more likely to respond with redirected anger or by avoiding all social contact, dogs are also susceptible to these reactions. As we discussed at length in the first chapter, dogs under the influence of strong emotions like fear and anger are often unable to make good decisions, no matter how much they might benefit from doing so. Pain is the same.

Dogs in pain are more likely to show more intense and sustained reactions than they might under normal circumstances. For example, a stranger coming to the house might cause a dog in pain to remain agitated and barking for several minutes, whereas under normal circumstances that same dog might accept the stranger very quickly.

Dogs in pain are much more susceptible to a well known behavioral phenomenon called "trigger stacking." A trigger is a stressor that brings out undesirable behavior in a dog, and stacking is the effect of multiple triggers coming at the same time or in close proximity to each other. Pain is a trigger - and a significant one at that! A dog who is healthy may be able to tolerate four or five triggers at one time without having a negative outward reaction, whereas that same dog may be able to tolerate only one or two triggers when in pain.

The fact is, chronic pain lowers tolerance for just about everything - other dogs, people, new experiences, stress, and so on - which makes it more likely that the dog will shut down or react aggressively. It's not hard to see how this might happen. Think about how you feel at the end of the day when you've struggled with an unrelenting headache. You may well project a normal demeanor to the world, but your tolerance for noise, frustration, and crabby people around you is likely to be severely reduced from your baseline.

A dog in pain is not in a frame of mind to learn because he is under the influence of his physical sensations and the related emotions, not conscious thought. As a result, any training which is undertaken is likely to work poorly, if it works at all. Or, the training may solve one problem only to have a new one emerge.

My Personal Experiences

As a dog trainer, I have seen a good deal of misunderstanding and suffering in the dog world as a result of undiagnosed illness or pain. I have seen dogs with joint disorders be asked to perform behaviors that were causing them pain. I have seen dogs be severely punished for unexpected aggressive behavior that was eventually diagnosed as a brain tumor. I have seen dogs with undetected cancer who were expected to tolerate small children climbing on them. I have seen dogs with bladder stones who were punished for toileting accidents in the house. I have seen dogs with separation anxiety be locked in crates for long stretches so that they could "get over it." I have seen dogs with sound phobias left outside during storms where they proceeded to claw their toenails off in their efforts to escape. In all of these cases, the owners felt bad when they become aware of the cause of their dog's problems. Unfortunately, the dog's experiences could not be undone.

Give your dog the benefit of the doubt. Physical and mental issues can be serious and debilitating. Our dogs deserve our best efforts to resolve their health problems. Simply assume that your dog is behaving to the best of his ability at any given time.

Summary

In the same way that we must be aware of the relationship between a dog's emotions and behavior when considering the appropriate solutions for behavior challenges, we must also consider the possibility that illness or pain may be driving a dog's behavior rather than conscious thought. If the pain or illness is managed, then the dog's behavior "miraculously" improves. While training can help all dogs, even those suffering from physical or mental pain, the reality is that our ability to learn and retain information is severely reduced if we're struggling with internal issues that need to be resolved.

If you have any reason to suspect pain, either mental or physical, talk to your veterinarian. If the issues appear to be largely emotional or mental, seek out a veterinary behaviorist to help you understand your options. Consider a trial course of medication if the dog appears to be in pain but the specific cause cannot be identified, and take note of the results. And do not be afraid to use medication for mental illness in dogs; much as with humans, mental suffering is real suffering, and we need to put aside our preconceived notions about mental illness and allow our dogs the help they need to allow them to lead a normal quality of life.

Notes

Chapter 3
Temperament of the Dog

While it is absolutely true that the things we do as dog owners can have an enormous effect on our dog's ability to learn and behave well, it is also true that each dog brings a genetic package to the table that influences his behavior. We cannot change a dog's basic temperament, so we'd be well served to work with a dog's innate tendencies rather than denying or fighting them. Just because you want your dog to be outgoing and sociable doesn't mean that he is. At the same time, just because your dog was bred to dig vermin out of the ground doesn't mean you should let him turn your garden into a minefield.

While the debate rages on about the relative importance of nature (innate temperament) and nurture (the dog's life experiences), for our purposes, let's just say that both matter. If you acknowledge and respect your dog's basic nature, it will be much easier to design your training to help him perform at his best. Start from a point of understanding, identify and develop a plan that respects both who your dog is and what you need to live together without conflict, and start your training! In this chapter we'll consider who your dog is, while later on we'll discuss how to develop a training plan that meets both of your needs.

Typical Temperament Traits

It would be well beyond the scope of this book to discuss the typical temperament for the 300+ breeds of dogs known worldwide, so instead, let's consider some of the things that dogs were bred to do, and how that might affect what we see in our homes on a daily basis. The easiest way to do this is by looking at breed categories. The United Kennel Club divides dogs into the following eight categories: Gun Dogs, Terriers, Herding Dogs, Guardian Dogs, Northern Breeds, Scent Hounds, Sight Hounds, and Companion Dogs.

A gun dog might be a retriever, a spaniel, or a pointer - and they're all different! Retrievers were bred to retrieve birds back to hand, so they tend to work close to their handlers with a lot of direction. As a result, they are typically handler dependent and highly cooperative. Spaniels are expected to find and flush the game in addition to retrieving it, so those noses tend to be going all the time! Meanwhile, pointers run far and wide - it's not a joke when hunters say they've picked up their dog ten miles from where they dropped him off! While pointers are also gun dogs, they are bred to work far afield; to do so, they need an enormous amount of energy and independence.

How does that translate to your home? The retrievers live specifically to fetch and carry things, like your socks! And sometimes they swallow those socks - sending you to the vet for expensive vet care that you probably wouldn't encounter if you owned a breed that had less of a desire to hold things in their mouths. Retrievers also tend to be very sociable. They have to be in order to get along with other dogs and their handlers in the field. While they aren't likely to bite anyone, they do have a tendency to be overly enthusiastic in greeting your guests. The spaniels are similar but their noses may be working overtime. And the pointers? Take out the obsessive retrieve and don't forget their desire to run in big open spaces whenever they can.

Next up we have the terriers, the brave explorers and hunters of the dog world! What kind of terrier gives up and runs home when the critter in the ground fights back? Not a very good one! That's why they were bred to enjoy a good fight and not back down, even when common sense would suggest it's time to throw in the towel. Terriers must be feisty and determined to succeed at their work.

How does that translate into a housepet? You may well get a curious, independent, tenacious digging machine. That rat living in your wall? On the plus side, it's been eradicated! Your dog persisted in the task of removing him while you were away at work. Unfortunately, you now have a gaping two-foot-wide hole in your plaster.

Then there are the herding dogs, who were bred to see every small change in their environment. A twitch of a lamb's tail or a change in the direction of the flock's gaze may provide critical information that will allow a good herding dog to head off disaster. Herding dogs must split their attention appropriately between the environment and the handler, to learn easily regardless of the handler's training skill, and to be able to problem solve as needed. Much of their skill is hard wired into them. For example, most working sheep dogs will round up critters obsessively; the training simply refines and polishes what is already there. Herding dogs tend to be extremely intelligent dogs who love to learn and who problem solve very well.

Having a smart dog who learns easily and wants to please might sound ideal, but there's a downside. Because they were bred to notice every change in the environment, they also see things that make them a little crazy - like every fly in your house. They tend towards obsessive compulsive behavior, but they have to! Being responsible for a flock of sheep is a full-time job. Who wouldn't be a bit neurotic if they felt responsible for keeping order at all times? These dogs struggle when they don't have enough to do, and it is often well beyond the capacity of the average pet owner to provide appropriate mental or physical stimulation.

How about the guardians? These watch dogs were bred to alert their owners early and often when something changed in the environment so that the humans could protect their stuff. What good is a watchdog who allows the bad guy to come in? A good watch dog is paying attention and keeping you informed!

Your guardian will tell you when the neighbor comes home. And your neighbor's neighbor. He also tells you when they leave. And for good measure, he tells you if he thinks that they might be thinking of leaving. Just in case. And while your dog is expressing his nature, you and the neighbors are thoroughly sick of listening to him. This is especially problematic if you live in an apartment, not on a farm. You may not need your dog to bark over every little thing that happens, but your dog's genetic code says otherwise.

And those scent hounds? They were bred to work in sociable packs, tracking game for hours. They have the most amazing noses and tons of perseverance! They have been bred to "bay" because they need to be heard by their handlers at great distances, sometimes miles away! Unfortunately, they will use that same voice at 2 AM when a raccoon shows up outside your bedroom window. What an awesome dog, letting you know about all the important things, and you're grumpy and ungrateful! But hounds tend to be both persistent and forgiving of irritable human behavior, so you can count on another wake up call tomorrow morning when the raccoon returns.

Scent hounds tend to be friendly, getting along with pretty much all dogs and people... including the burglar that just wiped you out. So your dog barks day and night at critters, but does not alert you when the bad guy robs you? Well, yeah. They're not bred to bark at people - and they certainly don't want to bite anyone!

Do you have your heart set on a sight hound? The ones who run like the wind with their long legs and elegant heads, following small game with single-minded determination? They amaze all of us with their speed and grace, whether on the trail of a bunny or running down the street after your neighbor's fleeing cat - equally appealing game for those sharp-eyed sighthounds.

These breeds tend to be quiet, low maintenance, and independent; all very attractive qualities in a low-key pet, but more than the minor challenge when you're trying to train.

Now let's consider the northern breeds - the ones who pull sleds. They like to run! And what direction are they running? Well, it's generally not towards you. Since they were bred to pull a sled, it's in their genetic wiring to pull against tension, which is rarely appreciated by the hundred pound owner who is being dragged around like a rag doll. On the plus side, they tend to be friendly, easy going, independent, intelligent dogs who manage to adapt to a wide range of living situations. That's if you can keep them in the house, because they are also the masters of escape.

Do you love the little toy dogs? The ones bred to sit on your lap for hours, not letting you out of their sight? They have a job too: to be your friend! And there they are, 24 hours a day, even when you just want to go to the bathroom by yourself. If you shut the door, they'll complain bitterly about being left out.

Obviously, some of these dogs have not done their original jobs for a very long time. In fact, some breeders have gone to some trouble to remove the original working qualities from their breed or have emphasized appearance over temperament, diluting some of the dog's original working characteristics. As a result, those dogs are probably going to have lesser degrees of their working traits. Still, genetic tendencies can be tenacious. Even a herding dog who has not had a relative herd sheep for fifty years is likely to retain some of the basic underlying temperament.

It can be frustrating when your dog insists on following you to the bathroom when you want some privacy. On the other hand, you enjoy your cuddly companion when you're lonely. Yes, your terrier seems determined to get scrappy with every dog in the neighborhood. But you love the antics, the curiosity, and the boldness that comes as part of his package. Your dog makes you laugh and you wouldn't have it any other way.

Sometimes, you don't have any information on your dog's likely temperament in the first place. If your dog is of unknown parentage, then you will not have the luxury of considering breed tendencies in terms of who your puppy will likely become as an adult. However, be aware that many qualities of temperament are actually present at a very young age. If you select a puppy who is reserved with strangers and mellow at eight weeks of age, there is a good chance that these qualities will follow that puppy into adulthood because sociability and energy levels are largely innate. By the same token, if you bring home a puppy with an enormous amount of curiosity, boldness, and energy at eight weeks, you may well have a bull in a china shop forever because those qualities are also largely innate. Select wisely.

Not All Dogs Fit the Mold

What if you bought a Doberman specifically because you heard they were bred to be guard dogs, but yours turned out to be fearful? He hides under the table when people come to your house instead of protecting your home. How did this happen? This brings us to the second aspect of genetics and innate temperament: individual variability. A great deal of variety can exist within the genetic code for a breed. Sometimes purebred dogs simply do not act like other dogs of that breed. There's nothing wrong with your dog, he's simply an individual with his own unique genetics!

Innate Temperament and Training

Does this mean that you should live with outrageous behavior? Since your terrier was bred to dig holes and find rats, does that mean that you should allow your dog to wreck your home? Should you not even bother trying to get a reliable recall on your nordic dog? Should you just give up and accept the 2 AM notification from your hound that a raccoon is afoot? And should you simply ignore the fact that your Doberman is cowering in a corner?

Of course not! Accepting innate temperament as a reality means recognizing and understanding who your dog is as a unique individual, but it does not mean sitting back and allowing destruction to occur!

Remember that nature (genetics) is heavily influenced by nurture (environment). And that's where training comes into play.

If you've got a northern breed that loves to run and pull, start your training immediately the day your dog comes home, not after you have a problem! Focus on those points you know he might struggle with. Recall! Waiting when you open the gate! Walking politely on a leash!

With your super social retriever puppy, you'll work on calm greetings from day one. No jumping up! No over-the-top screaming greetings when your puppy encounters people. You will focus on developing basic manners and not allowing significant bad habits to take hold.

And your dog with a guarding heritage? He needs to see everyone who walks through the door as a friend. Every person he meets on a walk is another friend! Cars pulling up? More friends! Don't worry, you won't "ruin" your guard dog. He'll still help you if you need it, but you'll also significantly increase the odds that you and your dog can live in harmony within our society.

None of this happens in a day - or a week. You'll work to mold your dog, slowly, gently, and persistently over a long period of time. The more your dog's innate package is in contradiction to what you want to develop, the more patience, time, and humor you'll need to have. And sometimes, you won't get there at all, so you'll need to settle for management over training, which we'll discuss in depth later in this book.

Summary

Take a moment to think about it. What was your dog bred to do? What aspects of that innate temperament do you like and not like? What choices can you make now to either prevent, change, or improve undesirable behaviors?

In the same way that you shouldn't buy a thick, long-coated breed that requires daily grooming if you suffer from severe arthritis, you probably shouldn't buy an independent, strong-willed dog if your primary interest is having an off-leash hiking companion. Start with a temperament that makes sense for your life and then mold it as needed. By working together, improving the qualities that you like, and slowly eliminating the ones that you find undesirable, you can end up with an excellent companion.

Chapter 4
Applied Training Skills

© Dae Grodin

As we have seen, each dog brings a package to the table that we must work with. But it's also true that our behavior can influence a dog's emotional, physical, or mental well being. Now the question is, how can we approach training in order to effectively work with our dogs? In this chapter, we'll change direction and consider the role of our applied training decisions. The concepts in this chapter are not specific to the dog. Rather, they are about the principles of learning that apply equally to all dogs - and indeed, to all species! In other words, this chapter is about good training.

When working to master excellent training, remember that perfection is never the goal; greater understanding over time is what allows us to improve our skills while giving our dogs the least stressful learning experience possible. Even if you make a lot of mistakes - and you will, because we all do - it's likely your dog will improve anyway. Dogs have been cooperating with humans for a very long time, and as a result, they have evolved to figure out what we want, even when we're doing a rather poor job of communicating with them. Of course, the better your skill as a trainer, the more rapidly you will make progress, and the less frustration you and your dog will experience along the way.

The Importance of Motivation

To change behavior, you need a way to motivate your dog. Most trainers focus on offering either food rewards or social rewards (like praise, approval, and playful interaction). Let's look at these options.

Social rewards are extremely important because they make positive behavior more likely. Dogs enjoy learning, and they particularly like to learn from people who seem to like them. Dogs enjoy our happy voices, our approval, our laughter, and even our positive facial expressions. Tell your dog he is amazing and watch what happens!

Take some time to figure out how you can make your dog "smile" at you. What can you do to cause your dog to wag his tail, relax his mouth, and "laugh" with you? Do MORE of those things when you want to see MORE of the behavior that your dog just showed you. If your dog just greeted your neighbor politely at the door, tell him that you are pleased! Pet his head, clap your hands, and smile - IF that is what he likes. If he prefers that you give him a belly rub, do that instead! Yes, your neighbor might think you're a little odd, but the ten seconds you spend telling your dog that you are pleased will pay off, both in improved behavior and in a better relationship with your dog. And anyway, it's a lot more fun than yelling "Dammit, get off!" for the same ten seconds. Isn't it better to look like a cheerful silly person than an irritable grump?

Social rewards are also important because they give you a way to reward your dog even when you don't have any cookies. But - and here's an important caveat - if you ONLY use social rewards when you don't have access to a cookie, over time your dog will be disappointed to receive your approval if he was hoping for a cookie. That would be really unfortunate.

To make that more clear, imagine if your boss regularly stopped by your office and told you that he appreciated you and liked your work. That would be awesome! You would look forward to those visits. But if your boss only stopped by your office and told you he appreciated you when he didn't have the money to pay you, those visits would come to predict bad news. Don't let that happen with your dog. Make praise and play a regular part of your interactions with your dogs so they remain positive events that your dog looks forward to.

Another reason we want to develop social rewards with our dogs is that, over time, our dogs come to appreciate the harmony that develops when working in a close relationship with you. If you are a significant part of your dog's life, he'll keep a much closer eye on you. He'll look to you for direction when he's unsure. He'll trust and like you more than if you only interact when you're annoyed or if you only give cookies when you're training. In short, social rewards and interactions develop your relationship with your dog.

Now that we've explored social rewards, let's consider food in training. If we use food, are we bribing dogs for good behavior? Will our dogs behave when we don't have the food? What advantages do food rewards bring to training that we cannot get with our voices and personal approval alone?

When we're trying to change behavior or teach our dogs what we want, food is, hands down, the most efficient way to communicate exactly what we want to happen, where we want it to take place, and how it should be accomplished. The reasons for this are simple. First, dogs like food! Hand it over as soon as you see a behavior that you like and you're very likely to see more of that behavior. Second, it's swallowed so fast that you can quickly practice that behavior again. Handing over a cookie is much quicker than praising your dog. Of course, you can use both! Four or five sits in a row for just a cookie, followed by a few for both cookies and praise, and then back to cookies. It's not as efficient as using just a cookie, but that pattern allows us to reap the benefits of both food and social approval to improve our training outcomes.

Food is excellent for teaching your dog where you want him. Dogs want to be where the cookies are. If a guest is due at your house and you keep feeding your dog some cookies on his dog bed, guess where your dog is going to hang out? On his dog bed! But if you want your dog on his dog bed in the living room and you keep giving him the cookies in the kitchen, you're unnecessarily complicating your training and confusing your dog.

Food can also be used to distract a dog - and sometimes, that's a good thing! For example, let's say your dog is so excited that your neighbor just came over that you can tell he's going to jump on your neighbor. Before your dog jumps, you can drop a small handful of food on the floor to distract him from jumping up. You get a couple of additional benefits here, too. In addition to not being able to jump up while eating off the floor, if your dog is not looking at the face of the friendly neighbor, he's much less likely to be attracted to her. This further reduces the odds of jumping up.

Over time, your dog will develop the habit of being calm and thinking about food when a new person walks in the door. That means that after a month of dropping food on the ground every time a person enters your house, your dog will have been conditioned to expect food and to think about eating and looking down. He will then be in a much better frame of mind to greet guests calmly, which means you just prevented an undesirable behavior from starting. Good for you! Now, go ahead and take it a step further. Feed your dog from your hand while new people pet your dog and he'll make the same calm association with getting petted.

How Motivators Work

Now that you understand the importance of motivation, there are a few things you need to keep in mind about how motivators work.

First, a motivator only works if your dog likes what you are offering. If you plan to reward good behavior with roughhousing (because you like it, or you think dogs should like it), but your dog hates it, then you're wasting your time. Actually, you're going beyond wasting your time if your dog does not like it; you're actually punishing your dog for being good. Think about that. It's not a good idea to antagonize your dog when he's being good, so make sure your dog likes the form of social interaction that you use. The same is true with food. If you offer hard dry biscuits and your dog sniffs them and carefully walks away, then you picked the wrong food motivator. Try using something else, preferably a treat that is small, soft, very tasty, and easily swallowed. If you think your dog doesn't like food, head for the fridge and get something worthwhile. Forget the dry kibble - get out the hot dogs. See how that works for you.

Second, to be effective, the amount of time between seeing the desired behavior and giving the reward must be extremely short. If your dog doesn't jump on your guest but you wait until after your guest is seated to go get a cookie for your dog, it won't do much for your training. Sure, your dog will enjoy the cookie, but he'll have no idea that you gave it to him because he didn't jump on your guest. Indeed, he may think it's because your guest decided to sit down. And while there is no harm in that, it's also not the training you had in mind. So be quick! A good rule of thumb is to reward the dog within two seconds of the good behavior, whether that's sitting when asked or not jumping on a guest. Most experienced trainers will have the cookies all ready to go before even opening the door for the guest.

Third, rewards only work if they are more salient to the dog than the alternatives at any given moment in time. Those alternatives can be of two basic types: attractors or stressors.

Attractors are alternatives that the dog cares about and wants to have. For example, your dog knows you have tasty cookies, but he sees a squirrel in the park. Which one is he likely to choose when you call him? An easy way to consider which alternative is likely to win is to assign a number value to it. For example, if you know that chasing a squirrel has a value of nine to your dog, then you need to come up with a cookie or reward that holds a value of ten. If you don't have one, don't put yourself in that situation. Instead, keep him on a leash, take him to a different park, or just don't call him when he's chasing a squirrel.

Stressors affect motivation differently because they will depress your dog's interest in what you have to offer. For example, if you take your dog to the local street fair and your dog finds the environment scary, the cookie that has a value of eight in your kitchen might now only be a two. If your dog won't eat in a given environment, then he's not in a trainable frame of mind. If he's so distressed that he cannot eat, he's also too distressed to learn. Leave before your dog tries to escape, lashes out, or shuts down in a puddle of misery.

Setting the Stage

Now that you understand motivation, let's talk about WHERE you are going to train your dog. You may remember from Chapter 1 that dogs in a highly emotional state are not in a good place to learn. Even if the dog is very happy, he will struggle to learn if his emotions are so heightened that he can't think clearly. Choose your training environments with care so he's not emotionally overwhelmed. The IDEAL place to train new behaviors is where nothing else is going on and your dog is engaged by your desirable motivators. Rather than taking your dog to dog school and teaching sit (where your dog is riveted by all of those new potential friends or enemies), how about teaching it in your kitchen first? This allows him to concentrate on your lessons, and he'll learn much quicker!

Next, you'll want your dog to understand that following your direction pays off in lots of places, not just in the kitchen where he first learned it. This is called generalization, which simply means repeating the training steps in progressively more challenging locations until your dog can succeed pretty much anywhere. First your house (so quiet), then your backyard (birds in the trees), then the front yard (people walking by), then the front of the grocery store (activity everywhere). When you finally get to dog school (dog and human distractions), your dog already knows the basics of what is being asked for, and the odds of success go way up! Since success breeds confidence in our canine learner, it is truly in our best interest to set the stage so that our dogs can win.

Rate of Reinforcement

When trainers talk about the rate of reinforcement, they are talking about how frequently the rewards should come. When teaching, you should use much more reinforcement than you think is normal or reasonable. The reason is simple. Dogs who are rewarded a lot are motivated, and motivated dogs learn much faster than unmotivated dogs. A high rate of reinforcement also allows dogs to avoid the frustration of wanting the reward but not knowing how to earn it.

Although rewards should come VERY frequently when the dog is learning, they can come much less frequently after the dog has learned the task. But even highly accomplished dogs will need the occasional morsel to keep them cheerfully optimistic.

Know What You Want

So what if your dog wants what you have, is focused on you, yet still is not performing the behavior? Then you can pretty well assume it's because you aren't teaching it in a way that he can understand. Think about it. If he wants what you have, is physically capable of performing, and understands your request, then there is no logical reason why he wouldn't cooperate. If he doesn't, well, you're doing it wrong.

So how do you do it right? Start by having a very clear vision in your mind of what behavior you want to see before you start training. Both dogs and humans do much better when we tell them what we want rather than what we don't want. For example, telling your child not to track muddy shoes throughout the house is reactive; it's already happened, and now you're annoyed. Instead, focus on teaching your child to take off his shoes and leave them on the porch. Now you can praise him for the clean floor rather than yelling about the footprints. That is an example of focusing on what you want - dirty shoes left on the porch.

Do the same with your dog. Let's say that your neighbor comes over and your dog wants to jump up. Instead of being upset AFTER your dog jumps up, ask yourself what you want your dog to do when your neighbor comes over. In this case, you want four feet on the floor. Excellent. Now you have something to train towards.

Know How to Get There

Of course, simply having the end goal in mind is not enough. There are many steps along the way, and the easiest way to teach (and learn!) is in tiny pieces. As your dog masters each piece, add another tiny piece until you have a finished behavior. This is called splitting behaviors.

Here's an example. Let's say you're trying to teach your child to read. You can't just hand him a book and expect him to read it to you. Instead, you need to start by teaching him the alphabet. But he can't learn all the letters at once, so you start by showing him a few letters. You keep working on a couple of letters at a time until your child can easily and fluently point to the correct letter. Then you'll need to add the sound of each letter, one or two letters at a time. Now, can your child still manage the alphabet when there are other children around? If your child can only perform under pristine conditions (like your quiet kitchen), he's not really fluent yet. If your young reader can easily identify the necessary letters, knows how to pronounce the sounds, can hear the sounds when they are spoken to him, and can do this even under less than perfect conditions, then he is ready to start learning how to read.

But how about when the child isn't quite ready to learn to read? Or is not interested in learning? Or is either excited by or fearful of what is happening around him? Or struggles with learning disabilities? Or has a headache? Or the parent asks for too much at one time? Or expresses frustration at failure? Or the lessons are simply too long and boring? What happens then?

The learner will opt out. He will not want to learn. If the process is not easy and highly reinforcing, it's not fun. And when learning is not fun, the learner will try to find ways not to do it. So instead of putting energy into learning, he'll put his energy into escaping the experience altogether. Will he learn anyway? Probably. Eventually most of us do manage to learn even under poorly designed learning set-ups. But it will take much longer than necessary and may sour your student on any future learning, not just reading.

What does all of this have to do with dogs? Well, all species follow the same basic laws of learning. Dogs need to be physically and emotionally ready to learn what you want to teach. They need to be interested and motivated. They need the right environment so they are not distracted, with generalization to new locations added as they show readiness. And finally, the materials need to be presented at a speed that fits the learner. When a dog is matched with a person who understands these pre-conditions and offers learning opportunities in small and digestible pieces, the dog will learn. When any of these conditions are not met, the learner is much more likely to struggle.

Choosing a Training Time

One of the most challenging realities of training is that learning takes place 24 hours a day, not just when it's convenient for you. If you want to raise a child who is polite, then you work towards that behavior at all times, not just when you feel like focusing on it. If you care about a behavior, then you must stay consistent with your expectations, looking for opportunities to reinforce good choices, and working hard to interrupt or prevent bad ones.

Inconsistency creates confusion and stress, so it's best to have simple rules that always apply. For example, if your dog jumps on you after you return from a long run, you may not care because you are wearing old clothes - especially if your dog's feet are dry. But if you've just returned from work in your nice clothes, you'll be upset if your dog jumps up - especially if he has muddy feet! Don't expect your dog to understand the difference. Simply have the same expectations at all times, regardless of the circumstances.

Let Your Dog Know When He's Done!

Some behaviors, like not jumping up, never end; we always expect our dogs to follow that rule. But when we cue our dogs to do a specific behavior, we don't expect them to do it forever. For example, let's say you asked your dog to go to his dog bed when a guest arrived, which he does. How long does he need to keep doing this? If you don't tell him, he will have to decide for himself. If you forget to let him know that he's done with that behavior, he will likely release himself. The problem with that approach is that next time he may release himself earlier, and earlier, and earlier - because you don't seem to care. The next thing you know, he's at the door with you when you greet your guests and you can't figure out what happened to your dog's training! Make sure that you let your dog know when a behavior is finished.

Punishment

Where does punishment fit into all this? It basically works the same way as reward-based training, but from the other side. Instead of getting more of what we want to see by rewarding it, the trainer works to see less of what she doesn't want to see by punishing it. If the punishment is scarier, more painful, or more bothersome to your dog than the behavior your dog wanted to engage in, then he will stop the behavior. If the punishment doesn't matter to the dog, then the dog will engage in the undesirable behavior anyway.

Punishment can be very tricky. The dog needs to understand why he's being punished. Consequences need to happen within a second or two if you want your dog to understand why he is being punished and what he should stop doing. In addition, your dog has to be in a good state of mind. If your dog is physically or mentally sick, then he cannot learn effectively. If his emotions or physical state are such that he's not in a place to learn, then it's not training all - it's simply the trainer being unpleasant.

Another challenge with punishment is that it doesn't tell the dog what you want him to do, only what you do not want. If the dog only knows what you do not want, he has to guess at what an acceptable alternative might be, and that's a stressful way to learn!

Finally, as often as not, the dog's trainer is also the owner, and that person may not be very good at training the dog. Indeed, having worked with many people and their dogs, I feel confident in saying that more than 95% of the time, when a dog is struggling to learn something, it's because of how the trainer is trying to teach it; the trainer isn't being clear and the dog has no idea how to do better. So while the trainer is muddling along, punishing the dog, the dog is simply scared and stressed because he has no clear idea what is wrong.

For these reasons and many more, I'm not a fan of punishment in training. There are too many unfortunate ramifications with its use that can be easily avoided by using reward-based training methods instead.

But Bad Behavior is Happening RIGHT NOW!

So if I don't advocate punishment, how should a person respond when the dog does something bad?

Let's say that you're cooking dinner and forgot to crate your puppy. You turn around to find that you've left your dinner roast on the counter - and your puppy has found it too! What do you do RIGHT NOW if you can't punish your dog? Interrupt the behavior. If your dog is about to engage in a highly reinforcing behavior like eating your dinner roast, then allowing it to continue makes it a lot more likely to happen next time.

Okay, but HOW do you interrupt a behavior? If you have a word that means "cookie" then use it! Yell "cookie!" and head to get one. If your dog follows you, then you win! Hand over the cookie and give some thought to how you'll ensure that doesn't happen next time. Then again, if your dog is holding your dinner roast, he may not be the least bit impressed by your offer of a little cookie. Now what? As with so many things, it will depend on the dog. The idea is to use the least amount of physical or mental force required to stop whatever is happening. For some dogs, a squeaked "Hey!" may be just enough to redirect the dog from what he's doing and to look at you. With other dogs, you may need to physically remove that roast from his mouth.

Regardless of what is happening or how you respond, the goal is to stop the dog's behavior and get the dog to re-orient to you. Once your dog is re-oriented, you can focus on what you do want! Praise the dog for THAT... and then do a little better with your management next time.

What you do NOT want is to actively scare your dog - you just want to stop what is happening at that moment with as little physical or mental force as possible. You know you applied the right amount of force if your dog stops what he's doing and orients to you. If your dog flattens or looks frightened, you got carried away.

And how about if you don't catch the dog in the act of misbehaving at all? Instead, you come home from your trip to the store and your roast is simply gone, eaten by your uncrated puppy? There's nothing to do - it's over and done. Simply keep your puppy out of sight until you're no longer angry, then move on.

These thoughts about handling misbehavior can be tricky to understand, so think about what you would do if you found a two-year-old eating a bowl of sugar in your kitchen. You would stop the behavior as quickly and as calmly as possible. In the future, you would keep the sugar out of reach. And if you simply found the aftermath but didn't actually catch the two-year-old eating the sugar, well, there's nothing to be done. Clean it up and manage better next time.

Interruption is a mild form of punishment. It is doing something that the dog finds distracting or unpleasant enough to stop what he's doing. Some trainers choose not to use it, while others feel that the benefits outweigh the risks, especially when an undesirable behavior is in process, harming the rights of others, or likely to be sufficiently reinforcing that not stopping it makes it quite likely that you'll see it again. You'll have to decide for yourself, but to do that, you'll need to understand the consequences of your decisions, so let's go back to our earlier scenario.

In order to get your dinner roast back, you trapped your dog in the corner and removed it from his mouth. What might happen now? If you're lucky, your dog will not take things off your counter again; he will have learned that food on the counters is not for him. If it's a neutral outcome, you'll be in about the same training place as you were before this event occurred. If you're unlucky, your dog will have learned to avoid you when he has something valuable and he thinks you might take it from him. So if you make the mistake of leaving food out again, your dog might grab the roast and bolt for the yard where he believes that you cannot catch him. If you're really unlucky, you will have taught him to run away any time he has anything and you even look in his direction - an unfortunate (and not at all unusual) result. And if you're really, really unlucky? Your dog will have no idea what caused you to come and grab him, so he will end up wary or afraid of you when you approach, even though that was never your intent.

How dogs respond to even the mildest punishment is totally dependent on the individual dog. In all cases, preventing misbehavior is a better answer than handling failure after the fact. Still, life happens, so you'll have to decide in the moment what seems to make the most sense for you and your particular dog. The more "normal" and less fragile your dog is, the more degrees of freedom you will have when it's clear that either training or management has failed. If you overreact, it's not worth beating yourself up; just try to do better next time.

Good Behavior is Happening RIGHT NOW!
One of the best training techniques is to get into the habit of paying attention and catching good behavior when it happens. Your dog didn't bark at your guest? Praise that! Your dog was particularly gentle when greeting a child? Praise that! Your dog saw that roast on the counter, licked his lips, but then walked away? Praise that... and what the heck! Get a cookie and hand it over to further reinforce your delight!

Humans are not in the habit of noticing and praising good behavior, but it's actually more important than discouraging bad behavior because it tells our dogs what we want to see. Be generous with your acknowledgment of good behavior. There is absolutely no downside and many potential benefits, not the least of which is a more polite dog who looks forward to hearing you tell him that he's wonderful!

Summary

In this chapter, we've talked about the training skills you need to bring to the table. This includes choosing appropriate motivators and offering those motivators at a high rate of reinforcement. You also need to select the right place and time to train your dog. And of course, you need to know what you want to see your dog doing, and how to break that picture down into small enough pieces that your dog can easily learn what to do. We've also talked about why I prefer not to use punishment, and what you should do when you catch your dog in the act of something naughty. Finally, we've discussed the fact that acknowledging behavior you like is always a better plan than discouraging what you do not like.

Speaking of a better plan, let's talk about that! What might be a good proactive plan for teaching your dog not to jump on your guests at the door? Using the principles of good training and behavior that I have laid out in this chapter, let's consider their practical applications in the next chapter.

Chapter 5
How to Design a Training Plan

In this chapter, we'll discuss how to set up a training session using the example of a dog who jumps on visitors at the front door. Keep in mind the good training techniques we discussed in the last chapter. Please note that we assume your dog is physically and mentally healthy, that his emotions aren't getting in the way of learning, and that his temperament is currently stable. If this is not true of your dog, you'll need to address those issues first.

Before You Start
Every good training plan starts by considering the basics. What do you want your dog to do? How will you motivate him to do so? Where will you begin working?

Your goal is to train your dog not to jump on guests at the front door. However, as we discussed in the last chapter, it's easier to think about what you WANT your dog to do instead of what you don't want. What does it look like when your dog isn't jumping on guests? There are many possible answers, but all of them include one simple idea: all four of your dog's feet remain on the floor. This is the behavior we'll be training for.

Now you need to choose a motivator. Let's say you choose kibble. As long as your dog really enjoys food AND simple kibble is sufficient to create a motivated and engaged learner, this will work just fine! Keep in mind, though, another dog might require something more enticing. Don't be afraid to pull out the hot dogs if you need to! Regardless of what you choose, you're going to be very generous with those snacks because you want your dog to enjoy this training, so have lots of them ready.

Next up: selecting a location. This one is easy. Because the behavior of jumping on guests at the front door tends to be very specific to this location, that is where we'll begin - at your front door!

Small Steps to Success

Now it's time to sit down and think about all of the small pieces that are required to teach your dog not to take your guests down as they come to visit. What might some of these steps look like? Well, that depends on your dog! Does he know what a doorbell is? If you have a brand-new puppy who has never heard a doorbell or seen a guest come through the front door, you're in a very different position than if you have a dog who hears the doorbell and goes crazy running around, barking, and leaping at the door!

Let's assume you have one of those crazy-wild dogs who has had experience with doorbells. You'll need to make the first steps smaller with those dogs. First, approach the door with your dog and drop some food on the floor. Do this a few times until your dog is looking around at the ground as you walk towards the door because he knows food is going to show up. Second, approach the door, put your hand on the door handle - without opening the door! - and drop the food. Again, repeat this process a couple times. Third, approach the door, open the door, and then drop food on the floor. Repeat.

If your dog begins to get overly excited at any point in this process, either go back one step and put more time into it, or stay at the current step until your dog is focused on the food instead of the doorbell.

By this time, your dog should be associating the door with food on the floor, which distracts him away from the door itself. His previous association with approaching the door - which included both the doorbell ringing and guests coming in - should be more neutral and less wild now.

Once your dog is approaching the door and is fairly calm as he does so, it's time to move on to the next step. (Incidentally, this is the step where your brand-new puppy can start since he has always been able to approach the door calmly.) Now you'll open the door, reach outside, and ring the doorbell. Immediately drop a small handful of food on the floor. Repeat this until your dog hears the doorbell and his tail wags and his ears perk up in anticipation of food.

Next, open the door, step outside, close the door behind you, ring the doorbell, open the door, and drop the food on the floor. Within a couple of days, your dog should be loving the sound of the doorbell - not because it means guests are coming over, but because it means food is about to appear!

Now it's time to recruit a helper. After all, the goal isn't to make your dog love the doorbell, it's to teach him not to jump on other people! Have your helper come to the door and ring the doorbell. You and your dog will approach the door - but not open it! Throw the food on the floor for your dog, and then repeat. This might sound a lot like the last step, where you went out and rang the bell. The difference is that your dog has a very keen sense of smell and has likely figured out there is someone else behind that door. This increases the challenge level! But remember, we want small steps.

Next, have someone ring the bell again, but this time you'll open the door and say hello. Do not let the person in, simply throw food on the ground, shut the door, and repeat. Why didn't you let the person in? Because each step is designed to keep the dog's emotional excitement low enough that he can still think. Plus, we want to create new patterns for dogs who've had prior experience with the doorbell. Instead of jumping on the person, we want him distracted by the food.

If your dog is ready to move on, things are about to get more interesting, but probably not more challenging. Have a person ring the doorbell and enter the house. As he does, throw the food on the floor. If your dog leaves the food to greet the person, instruct the helper to ignore the dog entirely while you point out the food on the floor. If that doesn't work, you'll need to increase the value of the food next time. Repeat this until your dog is more interested in the food than the person.

Now it's time to allow your guest to greet your dog. The person will arrive and ring the doorbell. You will open the door and drop food. The person will enter the house while you drop more food. As the dog is eating, your guest will quietly greet your dog. If that gets your dog too wound up, have your guest stop interacting with him and put more food on the floor. Repeat until you're happy with the greeting.

Now it's time to start generalizing the behavior. As mentioned in the last chapter, generalization means teaching your dog that the behavior expectation holds, even when the circumstances change. In this case, the changed circumstance will be new people at the door. Because having a new person at the door is a huge change, we're going to back up a few steps to make things a bit easier on your dog. Start at the point of having the new person ring the bell and opening the door, but without the person entering. Your dog will likely be able to progress through the remaining steps quickly.

Some trainers or handlers would add additional steps to make it even easier for the dog. And other trainers would approach it altogether differently. Remember, the behavior of "not jumping on guests" can take many forms other than "four on the floor." For example, many people teach their dogs to go to a dog bed or crate whenever the doorbell rings. The steps are the same as above except that your dog is taught to stay on the dog bed first, and then anywhere the directions above have said "throw food on the floor," you would throw food on the dog bed instead. Another method is to teach the dog to sit at the door. First you need to teach your dog to sit, then you'll teach your dog that the sound of the doorbell is the cue to sit. When the dog sits, you feed continuously from your hand. If the dog gets up, you stop feeding and wait until the dog resumes the sit. Another method is to teach your dog to grab a toy and hold it when guests enter through the door since many dogs do not jump when they are holding a toy.

And when does the behavior end? When you cue your dog with whatever word you choose to use, like "all done." Use that word as you walk away from the door and go back to whatever you were doing. If you put your dog on a stay, then make sure you end that behavior! If you sent him to his bed or a crate, let him know he's free to leave.

This training will not be accomplished in a single afternoon. For a young puppy with no prior doorbell experience, it will probably take a couple of weeks. For an older dog with a significant history of screaming and mauling at the door it might take a month or two if you devote five minutes a day to the activity. It's not a lot of time, but it does require consistency.

Do You Really Care?

So here's an interesting question to consider. Do you really care about having your dog greet your guests politely at the door? If you do, then train your dog. If you don't, find another way to spend your training time with your dog. Or maybe you do care, but you very rarely have guests over. If that's the case, maybe you shouldn't bother training it at all. Maybe you should just manage your dog when people come to the house.

The fact is, you should prioritize your training decisions according to your life and your needs. If you rarely have guests but you walk your dog every day, you might find that your five minutes a day is much better spent teaching your dog to walk nicely on a leash. Of course, everyone cares about having a dog who walks nicely on a leash, right? Nope. I have a ten-pound dog who pulls on a leash because I simply don't care. I did, however, care that he actively objected to having his nails trimmed, so I spent my five minutes a day working on that issue instead. In my situation, cooperating with nail trims was a priority over walking politely on a leash.

There are no "right" things to train; put your time into the skills that are important to you.

Training Never Really Ends

Once the behavior is trained, is that the end of it? No, because training is never really 100% done. If you followed the above steps, it is quite likely that your dog has developed an excellent habit at the door. If you take that for granted, though, over time the behavior will degrade, especially if your dog discovers joy in exploring the alternatives - like jumping up. Go ahead and carry the occasional cookie to the door when you're going to open it. That small maintenance step will save you a lot of grief.

Management

Management can prevent a lot of problems, but it does not change the dog's behavior. Instead, management either takes the issue off the table altogether, or it prevents a behavior from becoming a bigger problem than it might be with no intervention at all.

But what is management? It's any action that prevents your dog from engaging in a behavior. In the example used in this chapter, management would be putting the dog in a bedroom before answering the door. The dog is not being trained in proper greeting behavior, but he's also not bothering your guests. Sometimes management is the best option, especially if the dog's behavior poses an unacceptable safety risk. For example, if your dog does not enjoy the company of children and you know that children will soon be coming to your door, putting the dog away before answering the door is the simplest and safest solution.

Management can be done forever. You'll never train your dog not to jump up, but it's not a problem because you'll always put him in the bedroom. You might use management as a temporary measure until you have the time or inclination to train your dog. Maybe in a few months you'll have the desire to work through the training plan necessary to teach him to keep all four feet on the floor. Or, maybe not. It's not a moral issue; do what makes sense for your situation.

Train Your Dog or He'll Train Himself

If you do not teach your dog what to do, he'll likely train himself, doing more of whatever works for him and less of whatever doesn't.

Sometimes this isn't a problem. If your dog is mellow and not terribly interested in people, then odds are pretty good that your dog won't bother to jump on your guests; he may not even come to the door at all! In that case, you don't need to worry very much; you can put your training time somewhere else. Or, if your dog is very small, he might still jump on people, but no one cares much because of his size.

Sometimes, though, it's a huge problem if your dog trains himself. If your dog is larger, energetic, and enjoys guests, then not teaching him what to do and not managing his behavior is likely to become problematic. The chain of events from a person ringing the doorbell to a stranger entering is quite predictable. If your dog becomes anxious or excited when that happens, he'll select behaviors to express that, which could range from barking hysterically to jumping up gently to mauling the person with enthusiasm.

If you do not train an enthusiastic dog in proper greeting behavior, here's what's likely to happen:

Your guest shows up at the door and sees your adorable new puppy. Your guest makes a big fuss over the puppy, encourages him to jump up, and picks the puppy up to cuddle him right up near her face! This becomes your dog's expectation for greeting guests. A few months later, your cute little puppy is now a teenager, and he is not so cute or little anymore. That same guest now blocks the adolescent dog and tries to keep him off, but that only makes him more determined to climb up and greet the visitor. A few more months down the line and your dog is now an older teenager; he's full grown in his body but far from grown in his brain. Now your guest is irritated by the frantic dog leaping and jumping at her face, and you're embarrassed.

This is the point at which many owners use punishment, which could be anything from a mild scolding to encouraging the guest to bring her knee forcefully into the dog's chest. Because of the dog's prior history of reinforcement for jumping up, the dog is quite likely to ignore mild punishments, while his reaction to more severe punishments will vary depending on his innate temperament. Those reactions could range from becoming fearful of guests (because they predict punishment!) to becoming angry (pain incites anger in some dogs, especially the stronger tempered breeds) to absolute acceptance ("Oh! Stay off guests at the door!").

You can teach your dog what you want or you can allow your dog to train himself. Just remember that sometimes, what your dog teaches himself is not acceptable to society. It's your choice where you want to focus your training time and energy, so think carefully before you decide.

Summary
This chapter was designed to give you an example of how to set up a training session to take advantage of the good training techniques that were laid out in the prior chapter. However - and this is important - this example ignored the first three chapters in the book so that we could focus strictly on the issue of training. In order to do this, we assumed that the dog was in an emotional state that was conducive to training, that the dog's physical and mental well-being were in good shape, and that the dog's general temperament was sufficiently easygoing that the training would be likely to take. Unfortunately, that is simply not the case for many dogs who are expressing problem behaviors.

We will now turn our attention to these dogs. In Part 2, we'll look at real-life case studies and consider applied training programs for dogs who are not happy, healthy, and sound. This will go well beyond simple training techniques so that we can pull the whole package together.

Notes

Part Two:
Applied Case Studies

Now that you understand how your dog's behavior might be the result of his emotions, health, temperament, and the training you've provided him, it's time to practice applying these concepts!

In this second part of the book, we'll look at two very problematic behaviors - barking and not coming when called - through the lens of several different dogs. By doing this, you'll be able to see how to address a problem behavior by considering the root cause of the behavior instead of focusing on the symptoms. Keep in mind that these are just scenarios, not full case studies. Rather than providing long and detailed descriptions of the issues or laying out detailed training solutions, the focus will remain on showing the relationship between root causes and problem behaviors so you can become comfortable with the process of considering dog behavior from a deeper point of view.

Of course, there are many, many more problem behaviors than the two presented here, so we'll also spend time considering problem behaviors more generally. This will help you learn how to take all the information you've learned so far and apply it to an infinite number of problems!

Chapter 6
Problem Barking

Dogs do not need to be trained to bark; they bark as an innate quality of being a dog. Barking is how dogs communicate, and humans have a strong love/hate relationship with this reality. On the one hand, barking is valued when it alerts us to worrisome changes in the environment, or when our dogs bark to let us know that they need something, like a chance to eliminate outside! On the other hand, people tend to have very strong ideas about when barking is desirable and we often find that a dog's desire to bark exceeds our interest in hearing it.

Dogs who bark excessively are a common source of irritation for dog owners and neighbors alike, but since barking is innate to dogs, it can be a challenging problem to solve! Dogs come with wildly different tendencies when it comes to barking. Some dogs bark non-stop, others never bark at all. One human's "problem barker" is just right for a person living in different circumstances. It is helpful to keep in mind that excessive barking is a relative issue rather than an absolute one. Further, barking is often a symptom of other issues; if you can resolve the primary problem then the barking may simply resolve on its own.

Let's consider a variety of different barking dog complaints to understand the range of reasons dogs bark - and the range of solutions a human might try!

I. Kip
<u>Dog's Name:</u> Kip
<u>Owner's Name:</u> Diane
<u>Breed:</u> Terrier mix
<u>Age:</u> 2 years
<u>Health:</u> Kip appears to be in good health.

<u>Owner's Description of Complaint:</u> Kip is a terrier mix with a barking problem! Kip's owner, Diane, says that Kip is prone to bouts of hysterical barking at night. At night, if there is any change in the environment, no matter how minor, Kip will start hysterical, high-pitched barking while running through the house and out onto the porch, often staring into the yard where the real or imaginary threat resides. Random noises from the neighborhood often set off this barking. These episodes can continue for as much as twenty minutes at a time, happen most nights, and usually occur several times within a night. While Kip does bark during the day, it is not so disruptive or intense.

In the last few weeks, Diane has been receiving complaints from her neighbors, so she has to get this problem resolved or risk giving up her dog.

<u>General Temperament and Routine:</u> In general, Kip is friendly with people. Diane describes him as a happy dog who needs plenty of exercise to keep him calm and relaxed in the house. He plays with her other dog every day for exercise, and he enjoys going out for the occasional walk through the neighborhood. Kip does not appear to be a nervous dog in general, but he does have a strong watch dog tendency. Kip is loose in the house and has access to a doggy door into the yard.

<u>What has been attempted to solve the problem:</u> Diane has tried yelling at Kip to be quiet, but that made him worse. What currently works best

is for Diane to get up, pet and soothe him until he settles, and then head back to bed. While effective, it's also exhausting; Diane and her family need to get some sleep too!

Discussion: Darkness and night time tend to make dogs (and people) more suspicious. This is made worse because sounds are more noticeable due to lack of background noise. Both of these make "watch dog" barking more likely. Being loose in the house allows Kip to pace, which is very likely exacerbating the issue by activating his nervous system. Further, movement, nervous alarm barking, and being awake are all related; the more he moves, the more he is aware of his environment. The more he is aware of the environment, the more he barks. The more he barks, the more he is awake. The more he's awake, the more he moves, and so on…creating a highly reinforcing and undesirable cycle.

Conclusion: Kip does not have a barking problem; his problem is being awake at the wrong time.

Solution: Kip needs a new set of habits! Kip needs to stop being awake and patrolling the house at night. The simple solution is to crate Kip overnight, ideally by Diane's bed. He needs to learn that being crated in the bedroom means it's time to rest. The presence of his owner sleeping nearby should calm him and model sleep. It may also be useful to cover Kip's crate with a towel and to add some low level background noise to further reduce his ability to see and hear any changes at night that are likely to trigger his barking. Crating Kip at night also interrupts the cycle of movement, which reduces what he sees and hears in the environment, and further helps prevent him from barking. By breaking the old habits and starting new ones, the barking will reduce, and everyone's sleep will improve!

2. Flip

<u>Dog's Name:</u> Flip
<u>Owner's Name:</u> David
<u>Breed:</u> Hunting Labrador Retriever
<u>Age:</u> 10 months
<u>Health:</u> Flip has had two intestinal blockages, but is otherwise in good physical health.

<u>Owner's Description of Complaint:</u> Flip is a ten-month-old Labrador Retriever who was purchased as a hunting dog and companion for David. Flip's barking has become quite a problem for everyone in the neighborhood. When David first brought Flip home as a two-month-old puppy, Flip was left in the yard while David worked. By five months of age, Flip had started chewing pretty much everything he could find, including the side of the house, the lawn furniture, and the sticks and leaves under the trees.

After Flip experienced his second intestinal blockage and surgery to remove objects from his stomach, David decided to leave Flip in a crate during the day. Flip had been loose in the house at night, but David starting crating him overnight as well since he discovered that Flip was chewing the woodwork in the house while David slept. While crating solved the chewing problem, it seems to have started the barking problem. Flip will bark continuously during the day, and also for about a half hour when first crated at night before he falls asleep.

<u>General Temperament and Routine:</u> Flip is crated for about twelve hours during the day, and is let out by a neighbor for a short potty break in the middle of the day. He has been through one six-week-long puppy manners class. David works long days and is too tired to provide Flip with much in the way of exercise. Instead, in the evenings he usually watches TV with Flip nearby. David often attaches a leash to prevent him from getting into mischief in the house.

<u>What has been attempted to solve the problem:</u> David used a bark collar at the recommendation of Flip's breeder. Initially that seemed to

work, but Flip started chewing on the base of his tail within two days of wearing the collar, so David decided to take it off.

Discussion: Young, active dogs cannot be expected to live in a crate for twelve hours during the day and then again for eight hours overnight, even with a potty break. How much exercise a dog needs will be highly dependent on the age and breed of the dog, but Flip needs significantly more exercise if he is to accept the total amount of crating he is experiencing. Punishing him with a bark collar may solve the symptom (barking), but if the underlying cause of the barking is not addressed, then Flip is bound to start an alternate activity to relieve the boredom. In this case, Flip began chewing on his tail.

Conclusion: Flip does not have a barking problem; he is simply a young dog who needs more stimulation and exercise!

Solution: Crating Flip is a good idea because it is not safe for him to be randomly destroying the yard and developing intestinal blockages, but he needs something to do in that crate! David should feed him his meals out of puzzle toys and give him long lasting chews to keep him busy. He also needs to be released from his crate for more than a bathroom break in the middle of the day; he needs real exercise!

Because Flip is friendly with everyone, David can easily arrange for someone to come in daily to ensure that Flip gets plenty of physical exercise, either by playing a high-energy game of fetch in the yard or by taking a long walk through the neighborhood.

In addition, Flip needs to use his brain because physical exercise is not enough! At night, David can train Flip, both on practical exercises like his recall and hunting skills, but also on tricks and impulse control exercises.

3. Bandit

<u>Dog's Name:</u> Bandit
<u>Owner's Name:</u> Dana
<u>Breed:</u> Cattle Dog mix
<u>Age:</u> 2 years
<u>Health:</u> Bandit appears to be healthy.

<u>Owner's Description of Complaint:</u> While normally very quiet in his home, Bandit barks at dogs and people when he is taken for walks through the neighborhood. Even though he has never attempted to bite anyone, Dana is worried about passing other people on the sidewalk. She tightens up the leash for safety when she sees someone coming, which causes Bandit to start lunging and barking almost immediately, making the problem much worse. Dana is at the point where she no longer wants to take Bandit out of the house unless she can stop his barking and lunging at people.

<u>General Temperament and Routine:</u> Bandit was disinterested in new people and dogs from the day he came home, preferring to hang out with Dana. The barking and lunging didn't start until Bandit was over a year old, after Dana started taking him to a local elementary school for socializing with people and to a dog park to meet other dogs. Bandit never enjoyed either of these places, hiding under chairs at the dog park and trying to avoid the people who wanted to pet him at the school. On a few occasions, Bandit was overwhelmed and growled and lunged, at which point Dana decided to stop the socialization efforts. Because Dana works from home, she is able to take him out for several walks each day. He receives additional exercise playing ball in his own yard.

<u>What has been attempted to solve the problem:</u> Dana has tried feeding him cookies while strangers approach and pet him.

<u>Discussion:</u> People and dogs make Bandit nervous. The socialization trips where he was handled and greeted against his will exacerbated

his discomfort. Bandit found a strategy that was effective at keeping people away: barking and lunging.

Dana's efforts at socialization were certainly well-intentioned, but also misguided because she did not honor his emotional discomfort. Rather than teaching Bandit that dogs and people would respect his desire to be left alone, he learned that he would be forced to interact regardless of his opinion. By removing his choice to leave, and by repeatedly visiting places that made him fearful, what started as a generic disinterest in dogs and people became fear and worry.

You cannot change innate temperament through socialization or forced exposure to things that frighten a dog. Good socialization is simply exposure at levels the dog is comfortable with, along with choice about when or if to interact. Good socialization does not require interaction. In the same way that a two-old-child who is fearful of new people is simply ignored and allowed to become comfortable on her own, a young puppy who is fearful should also be exposed to a variety of experiences from a safe distance, but not forced to interact with either people or dogs. Once the puppy is ready, he should be allowed to explore at his own pace. Forced socialization rarely ends well. Unfortunately, this is a common socialization strategy used by new dog owners, and acquired reactivity can be a common result.

Conclusion: Bandit does not have a barking problem; he has a fear problem.

Solution: Bandit barks to keep dogs and people away. If Dana increases the distance between Bandit and the dogs and people who make him nervous, then she can avoid the barking behavior, ultimately breaking the cycle of "see new person - bark - person stays away". Because Bandit's temperament as a puppy was to be neutral towards new people, it's quite likely that he will become neutral again when he realizes he no longer needs to bark to protect his space. In addition, when Dana takes on the job of protecting his space for him, he'll be able to relax and enjoy his outings without being on high alert about what might happen.

In addition, Dana should bring food on his walks and give him random cookies to help him to enjoy his walks more. Strangers should not give him cookies; he might be lured out of his comfort zone. Once he has swallowed the cookie, he could realize he is too close to the stranger for comfort and bark at the perceived threat, practicing the exact behavior that Dana is trying to extinguish. When Dana sees a person approaching, she should cross the road so there will be no interaction. Instead of using a tight leash to pull him away, she should hold a cookie in front of his nose to help guide him further away. It's important to avoid a tight leash because this tension often makes dogs want to pull forwards, making the barking/lunging cycle more likely. The use of a front clip harness that discourages pulling will also help prevent the tendency to pull and bark.

Dana can restart her socialization plan with Bandit if she wishes to help him become more neutral towards new experiences - but with three caveats. First, Bandit may always decide when he wants to leave. If he tries to turn around and head home or back to the car, then she is to go with him. Second, Dana must not allow anyone to approach Bandit; Bandit gets to decide if he wants to approach others. Third, Dana must keep Bandit far enough away from the people or dogs that he is comfortable simply sitting and watching in a relaxed manner. Anything closer than that, and he'll be practicing his fear response. The goal is exposure without forced interaction.

4. Zoey

<u>Dog's Name:</u> Zoey
<u>Owner's Name:</u> Lorra
<u>Breed:</u> Portuguese Water Dog
<u>Age:</u> 18 months
<u>Health:</u> Zoey has no known physical health problems.

<u>Owner's Description of Complaint:</u> The problem starts when Lorra goes to work; Zoey will refuse to go in her crate. Although Lorra feels

terrible, she has to push Zoey into the crate in order to leave the house. Zoey used to whine and pant when Lorra would get ready for work but over time that has become more pronounced. Now Zoey is barking loudly as soon as Lorra takes her clothes out of the closet.

When Lorra returns home from work, Zoey's paws and crate pad are covered in drool. Zoey will not have touched her puzzle toy, but she usually eats the food within a few minutes of Lorra's return. Zoey is wild and frantic when released from her crate but settles down relatively quickly.

Lorra reports that Zoey will often sleep in her crate and entertain herself with her chews and puzzle toy while Lorra watches TV in the evenings, so Zoey does not appear to be afraid of the crate. Zoey also sleeps in her crate at night with no barking at all.

General Temperament and Routine: Zoey is the love of Lorra's life! She gets long walks every day when Lorra returns from work, and multiple walks on the weekends. She also gets plenty of training and mental stimulation on a daily basis because Lorra enjoys training Zoey to perform a wide variety of behaviors.

What has been attempted to solve the problem: Lorra was encouraged to leave lots of puzzle toys and chews in Zoey's crate, so she increased the quantity and variety of options, to no avail. Zoey refuses them all until Lorra returns home. She has tried covering the crate, placing it in different rooms in the house, and having a house sitter come midday to let her out. While Zoey is happy to see the house sitter and to go for a walk, the house sitter doesn't want to come anymore because it is so difficult to get Zoey back in her crate when the visit is over.

Discussion: Dogs who drool and refuse food in their crates, but only when the owner leaves, are almost always under the influence of fear or even panic. The frantic behavior when Lorra comes home is an expression of relief, though it can be quite difficult to manage if the dog is also clawing and accidentally hurting her owner, which is common.

<u>Conclusion:</u> Zoey does not have a barking problem; she has a separation anxiety problem. Barking is a symptom that cannot be treated until the underlying emotional causes are addressed. At that point, the barking may resolve on its own, or additional training may be required.

<u>Solution:</u> Separation anxiety is often the result of a mental imbalance. Appropriate treatment and medications require the help of a veterinarian, ideally a veterinary behaviorist. These professionals can help the dog feel better while a training plan is instituted to begin to change the dog's habits and behavior patterns. If your regular veterinarian is not comfortable treating mental disorders, ask for a referral to a veterinary behaviorist or call the nearest university with a veterinary program.

5. Cain

<u>Dog's Name:</u> Cain
<u>Owner's Name:</u> Mark
<u>Breed:</u> Mastiff
<u>Age:</u> 3 years
<u>Health:</u> Cain has chronic weight issues as well as hip and elbow dysplasia. Medication is used for more extreme episodes of joint pain, but not on a regular basis. Cain is on a diet to help manage his weight.

<u>Owner's Description of Complaint:</u> While Cain is very sweet and loving with people that he knows, he also aggressively barks and lunges at people who walk through the front door, and he will continue to bark at new people for extended periods of time after they enter the house. This problem seems to have escalated as he reached maturity and has become increasingly worse over the past six months. Cain does not show aggression on his walks or away from the house.

<u>General Temperament and Routine:</u> Cain is a very calm and loving dog with his owner, though Mark has noted that Cain seems more irritable now that he is on a strict diet to control his weight. This irritability is primarily expressed as mild guarding of any edible chew objects. Mark

takes Cain for a walk every morning, but he is not comfortable walking for long distances due to his dysplastic joints.

What has been attempted to solve the problem: Cain is brought to the front door on leash but the tension on the leash appears to have increased his aggressive displays rather than reducing them.

Discussion: Cain is a Mastiff, which is a very large and powerful dog bred for generations for their guarding ability. Indeed, Mark acquired Cain when he moved into a neighborhood with high rates of crime in order to feel safe. While Mark feels safe, he does not feel that he can have guests come to his house.

Due to Cain's chronic health conditions and his tendency to limp after even moderate exercise, it would be a good idea to talk to the vet to ensure that his pain is being appropriately managed. Mark has also noticed that Cain's restricted diet seems to be having a negative effect on his behavior as well, and while there is relatively little that can be done about that except to offer "filler" foods to make him more comfortable, it needs to be understood that hunger and pain can both have a significant negative effect on aggression.

Conclusion: Cain does not have a barking problem; he has an aggression problem, probably rooted in his territorial nature and possibly exacerbated by the ongoing experience of pain.

Solution: Cain's barking behavior is rooted in significant aggression and should be managed until a professional trainer can offer specialized support. When working with aggression, in particular with large and powerful breeds of dogs, learning from a book is not appropriate.

For safety reasons, Cain needs to be crated when people come to the house. A first step in his training plan would be to feed Cain his meals in his crate to ensure a very positive association with his crate. Next, under the supervision of a professional trainer, Mark should work on the doorbell training exercise as described in Chapter 4 to reduce his aggressive response to the doorbell, but instead of training Cain to stay by the door, Mark should teach him to go to his crate when the doorbell rings. If necessary, Cain could be crated in a part of the house or garage where he can't see or hear the guests. Guests should not be allowed to approach him or his crate and should be instructed to ignore him altogether.

6. Britta

Dog's Name: Britta
Owner's Name: Carolyn
Breed: Sheltie
Age: 2 years
Health: Britta has no known health issues.

Owner's Description of Complaint: Britta barks a lot! Britta barks when Carolyn comes home or when she leaves. She barks in the yard when she sees something move, and she barks when she hears people walk by on the sidewalk. She barks when it's time to eat, time to go for a walk, time to come in the house, and time to go out. She barks when she plays with people and dogs. She barks when people are home, and she barks when she's alone. When Carolyn leaves the house during the day, the neighbors report that she'll bark on and off for as much as twenty minutes out of every hour all day long. Everyone is tired of listening to her!

General Temperament and Routine: Britta is a high-energy dog who loves to go for walks, ride in the car (barking out the window), and hike with the family. Playing ball is one of her favorite activities! She has a doggy door and comes and goes as she pleases when the family is gone for the day.

What has been attempted to solve the problem: The family tells her to be quiet, but it has no impact on Britta's behavior. One of the neighbors sprayed her with a water hose over the fence, and while that scared her into running away from the fence, it did nothing for the barking problem.

<u>Discussion:</u> Britta does not show any signs of distress with her barking; it appears to be tied strictly to arousal. And Britta becomes aroused very easily. Britta barks whether excited and happy because her family has come home, or in response to any simple change in the environment, like leaves falling from the trees! Because she barks at just about everything, it seems that her barking is an expression of emotion - any emotion!

<u>Conclusion:</u> Britta is an emotional barker.

<u>Solution:</u> Britta needs a few changes to her daily routine. First, it would be extremely helpful if Carolyn automatically offered her a toy or ball in any situation where arousal is likely to occur. If Britta's mouth is full, it is unlikely that she will bark. To teach this, Carolyn can hand her the toy and then they can go to the yard and play ball. Over time, Carolyn can delay the playing and emphasize the carrying of the toy to keep her quiet. Any time Britta becomes excited, Carolyn should encourage her to find and carry a toy. If Britta is not interested in a toy, Carolyn could drop food on the ground and encourage her to find it in order to redirect her from excitement and barking to searching for food and being more calm.

Second, Britta should not have a doggy door. Since she is fully housebroken, she should be contained in the house during the day so she is much less likely to receive constant stimulation from the environment. She should also be contained in a much smaller part of the yard that has a visual block on all four sides; the less she sees in the world as a whole, the less she'll bark. In exchange, she can be left with puzzle toys that contain food to occupy her.

Third, when engaged in formal training activities, it is recommended that food be used to motivate good behavior, since food tends to calm a dog's behavior.

The fact that Britta's barking is tied to pretty much all arousal and is not symptomatic of a deeper concern is positive for her well being, but at the same time she cannot be allowed to endlessly disturb the neighbors. Setting up her environment to make barking less likely or giving her things to hold when barking is inevitable will reduce her barking considerably.

7. Dante

Dog's Name: Dante
Owner's Name: Stacy
Breed: Australian Shepherd
Age: 3 years
Health: Dante has no known health issues.

Owner's Description of Complaint: Stacy says that Dante controls the house with his barking. He barks at them in particular, not at the world in general. He barks when he wants to go outside and when he wants to come back in. He barks the entire time his meal is being prepared. He barks when he knows it's time to go for a walk. Dante has been barking at them since the day he came home at eight weeks of age, and it has gotten worse and worse over time. Dante is crated during the day with chewies to occupy him and he does not bark at that time. He also doesn't bark when he is alone in the yard, nor does he bark excessively when guests come to the house.

General Temperament and Routine: Dante is a confident, outgoing, and happy dog. He gets plenty of exercise on a daily basis. He attended a basic obedience class, but no one followed through on his lessons at home.

What has been attempted to solve the problem: In an effort to stop Dante's barking, the family has tried to ignore it, but he gets even louder. On the advice of a friend, they tried waiting him out. After he barked continuously for ten minutes, becoming more agitated as time went by, they gave in to his demands to avoid complaints from the neighbors.

<u>Discussion:</u> Dante's behavior started early, and may have resulted from either one cause or a variety of causes working together. For example, he may initially have been lonely when crated, so he barked out of distress. Or he may have been frustrated at being crated, so he barked out of anger. Or he may have been hungry and excited at meal times, so he barked out of frustration and hunger. Over time, his barking either worked directly (his family released him from the crate to stop the barking) or as a coincidence (the family planned to let him out of the crate or feed him anyway, and he just happened to be barking at that time). At any rate, Dante seems to have made the connection between barking and getting what he wants, regardless of the underlying emotional reason for barking in the first place.

It's important to note that if a dog's emotional reactions are mild, he will be able to make connections between specific behaviors that he does (barking) and the reactions of others (giving him what he wants). If a dog's emotional reactions are stronger, it would be much harder to make those connections, and even if he could make the connections, the experience of the emotions themselves would be the primary driver of his behavior.

<u>Conclusion:</u> Dante has learned to get things that he wants by barking.

<u>Solution:</u> Dante's training needs to be approached from multiple angles. First, Dante will need to learn alternative behaviors that work for him instead of barking. For example, first Dante can be taught to earn a cookie with a polite sit. If he sits, he gets a cookie. If he barks, Stacy leaves and the cookies are returned to the shelf. The goal is that he "wins" 90% of the time, so Stacy must be fast about giving Dante that cookie after he sits but before he starts barking. If he doesn't sit, Stacy should lure him into the sit with a cookie instead of waiting him out as he will likely bark. When Dante is confidently sitting on cue and getting his cookie, that behavior can be taken to areas where he tends to show high levels of arousal, like his food preparation area or where his leash is attached for walks. Within a few days, Dante should be able to sit politely when he wants a cookie from his owner - without barking.

While this training takes place, the patterns that lead to feeding and walking should be broken. For example, rather than having him in the house barking while food is prepared, he should be put in the yard and fed directly upon coming in the house. He should go for walks through a different door than normal to avoid the habitual barking that is now the norm.

The next step is to put these pieces together. Dante is in the yard while food is prepared and then brought in the house. Before the food is placed on the ground, Dante is cued to sit. If he sits, the food is put on the ground instantly. If he barks, he is returned to the yard. On the next attempt, it will be made easier; he can be cued or even lured with a cookie in the hand.

Over time, the goal is to replace demand barking with polite sitting to get Dante things that he wants. Barking will be punished by either removing Dante from the room if he barks, or by having Stacy leave for a short break before returning to try again. Always remember that we want much more success than failure, so Stacy needs to set up for that!

Why not simply ignore demand barking? With a long and strong history of success, Dante is likely to work himself up into a frenzy - well past the point of any thinking at all. If he becomes frantic, learning new behaviors becomes much harder, and the amount of time that Stacy might have to wait for him to stop barking would be well beyond her tolerance. This is particularly true since she has tried waiting him out in the past only to give in. Instead, substitute "demand sitting" for barking. Only when the sit is well established should Stacy add in extinction for the barking. This means that once Dante knows that sitting works, Stacy can simply leave the room or remove him from the room if he barks. Since he has an alternative behavior that he knows will work, it will occur to him to offer it as long as he doesn't get so frustrated that all conscious thought turns off.

This pattern of training should be applied in all areas where his demand barking has become a problem.

Summary

While the above examples are far from thorough case studies, they illuminate the wide variety of reasons why dogs exhibit a problem behavior like barking. As we look back over these dogs and their problematic behavior, we can see that of all of them, only Dante has been "trained" to bark as a conscious choice that he controls. In all of the other cases, the barking either results from - or is exacerbated by - other issues, ranging from emotional or physical distress to sheer excitement and joy.

In a more formal analysis, details could easily be revealed that would further illuminate the situation. For example, we might learn that the dog behaves very differently with different members of the household, or that the problematic behaviors only occur in one location and not others, or that the dog had a traumatic experience early on that didn't seem relevant before. It's also possible we don't know about the things that might be contributing to the problem since they only happen when no one is around. As a result, it's important to evaluate the solution that is chosen. That issue of evaluating success or failure will be discussed in more depth in Part 3.

Chapter 7
Recall Issues

© Sharon Gretch

Few things frustrate dog owners as much as a dog who does not come when called. While many owners spend time on this critically important skill right from the start, sometimes the training doesn't work out as planned. The dog comes when he wants to, or when you have a cookie, or when there is nothing else happening. But when it's freezing cold outside and you need to go to work, a game of keepaway rather than returning to the house at your request can be maddening!

There are a wide range of reasons why dogs do not come when they are called and, at root, they all go back to the basic reasons laid out in the first part of this book. Either the dog cannot respond because of his emotions, he is physically or mentally unwell, or he simply hasn't been trained properly. This chapter will offer brief case studies of several different dogs and consider these possibilities. In each case, the owner is frustrated by the dog's lack of recall, but the appropriate solution for each dog is totally different!

I. Tiffany

<u>Dog's Name:</u> Tiffany
<u>Owner's Name:</u> Brenda
<u>Breed:</u> Havanese
<u>Age:</u> 10 months
<u>Health:</u> Tiffany has no known health issues.

<u>Owner's Description of Complaint:</u> Brenda purchased Tiffany as a companion for her family. She was looking for a small dog who would be friendly with her children, and in most regards, the family got exactly what they wanted. The kids play with Tiffany all the time! Brenda reports that the kids' favorite game is chasing Tiffany through the house. The family loves her as a family companion, but they are having a major problem with her recall. Tiffany won't come when called. Indeed, lately she runs off as soon as they look at her!

Tiffany's behavior is causing a good deal of irritation for everyone. She seems to think recalls start a game of keep away. Her family knows that it's much better to get Tiffany to come to them rather than having to catch her, but sometimes they don't know what else to do.

Tiffany's lack of recall is also causing problems for her housebreaking. After they let her out, they can't get her to come back in, so they are letting her outside less often. Now she is having accidents in the house even though she appeared to be potty trained a few months ago.

<u>General Temperament and Routine:</u> When Tiffany first arrived in their home, she had no recall issues at all. Tiffany used to follow the family closely through the house, so they saw no reason to teach her a formal recall or to institute special training.

Tiffany is generally loose in the house during the day. She is pottied in the backyard and called in a few minutes later. For exercise, the kids play chase with her in the house or yard. They also take her places like the local park, but they keep her on leash because of her recall issues. If no one is home during the day, Tiffany is crated. She appears comfortable in her crate and does not have accidents.

What has been attempted to solve the problem: To catch Tiffany, the kids trap her in a corner and then pick her up. This had been working, but she's started urinating when they come close, and at least once she growled when a child reached to pick her up.

Discussion: There are several issues that need to be resolved, including the games that the family plays, Tiffany's reaction to the approach of a human, and Tiffany's response to a recall cue.

The game of "chase the puppy" can be extremely problematic for young dogs for two reasons. First, it teaches the puppy that running away when a person approaches is a fantastic and fun game - way more fun than coming to the owner! Second, sometimes puppies get scared when playing the game because they become unsure if they are being chased for fun or hunted down. At best, that creates uncertainty in the puppy; at worst, it creates an emotional reaction of fear.

The second issue is how Tiffany currently perceives the approach of a human. Because she has been trapped and caught against her will, she is now uncomfortable when she is approached. That fear response has begun to trigger submissive urination. Tiffany needs to develop a new association that is devoid of fear when humans approach. Indeed, she needs to look forward to the approach of people!

And finally, the family relied on Tiffany's puppy nature rather than formal training to create a recall. It is common for puppies to have a natural recall because they rely on the security of a person, but as they gain in confidence they become much less likely to stay close. That is why training needs to start before that teenage stage hits! Tiffany needs to be taught the appropriate response to a recall cue so that she can develop a habit of cooperation!

Conclusion: Tiffany has been trained to run away and to fear the approach of people.

Solution: The games of chase must stop - or at least, chasing Tiffany must stop! Instead, family members should practice facing Tiffany (as if they are going to chase her), throwing a cookie down between the two of them, and then running off so that Tiffany chases them! When Tiffany catches up, she can receive another cookie from the person's hand. Over time, the family can practice walking closer and closer to her before running away, always giving her a cookie and then leaving again without reaching out to touch her or catch her.

To eliminate the issue of having to catch Tiffany after she potties in the yard, she should go outside on leash. She should also receive a cookie each time she returns to the house so she looks forward to coming back in. Eventually the leash can be removed, but the cookies for returning should remain for some time.

Finally, it's time for Tiffany to learn what "come" means! When Tiffany is nearby, her family should call her, hand her a cookie, and then send her off to continue whatever she was doing. This teaches her that being called doesn't mean she is going to be picked up or stopped from having fun, it simply means that she will get a treat. Over time, the family can start touching her collar and attaching the leash before giving her the cookie, only to remove the leash and let her be free again! Soon Tiffany will see that she can have her cake and eat it too; she gets both a free cookie when she comes when called, and she gets to go back to doing whatever she wishes.

2. Puzzle
Dog's Name: Puzzle
Owner's Name: John
Breed: Beagle
Age: 5 years
Health: Puzzle was hit by a car and sustained minor injuries a few months ago, but has no other known health issues.

Owner's Description of Complaint: Puzzle was adopted from a local shelter a year ago. John was looking for a hiking companion, and he knows that Beagles like adventure! Puzzle is a great dog in every way except one. John wanted a dog he could take hiking off leash, but Puzzle almost never comes when called if they are out on a trail. When Puzzle goes out for a hike, his nose hits the ground and never seems to come up again!

A few months ago, Puzzle did not respond to a recall cue and was hit by a car. John had been running after him and calling the whole time, but Puzzle did not listen. Indeed, he seemed oblivious to John. Even though Puzzle was not badly hurt, the event scared John enough that he decided to seek professional training even though he has always taught his prior dogs to come when called on his own.

John states that Puzzle doesn't really run away, but simply follows a smell without looking back. Puzzle doesn't seem to notice other things when he's following a smell, not even John or the cookies that John carries.

General Temperament and Routine: Puzzle doesn't show much interest in playing ball for exercise, but he looks forward to his two daily walks around the neighborhood. He also spends long periods of time in his yard barking at and chasing the squirrels in the trees. John has no close neighbors, so this behavior is not a problem, and he figures it provides Puzzle with both exercise and mental stimulation. Puzzle is quiet and clean in the house. He's the perfect pet - except for the recall!

What has been attempted to solve the problem: John carries treats on all of his hikes and gives them to Puzzle, but this only works if Puzzle is within a few feet of John. Otherwise, Puzzle seems oblivious to recall cues. This is particularly frustrating to John since this is how he successfully trained his prior dogs.

Discussion: Puzzle is a Beagle, a breed of hound that has been bred for generations to obsessively follow the trails of game independently, persistently, and at great distances from their handlers. Puzzle's innate desire to explore and use his nose is so motivating that John has nothing to offer that can begin to compete. In a case like this, training a reliable emergency recall is appropriate, but it needs to be understood within the context of management and safety. Puzzle simply cannot be allowed off leash unless he is in a safely contained space.

Conclusion: Puzzle's innate temperament is likely to make a solid and reliable recall very difficult to attain.

Solution: John needs to learn excellent management skills. He also needs to train an emergency recall.

In this case, management means that Puzzle needs to remain on leash. In the same way that we hold the hands of toddlers in public to ensure their safety, John needs to accept that Puzzle must be on leash, even in the woods where he would like to let him off leash. The risk of having Puzzle get lost or injured is simply too great to approach it any other way. A dog's genetics and temperament will have an enormous influence on a dog's interests, and Puzzle's interest in using his nose in the woods is far greater than his interest in anything that John has to offer.

John also needs to develop an emergency recall. To do this, each day John needs to get several pieces of Puzzle's absolute favorite food, say the name of the food (like, "Cheese!"), and rapidly feed it to Puzzle when he shows up. This training should start when Puzzle is doing nothing else and there are no distractions, until the magic food word causes Puzzle to come running from absolutely anywhere in the house at any time. When that is reliable, the emergency recall training should continue under higher distraction situations - but nowhere that Puzzle might decide not to listen. The goal is that Puzzle should develop an extremely strong habit of running directly to John when he hears the special food word. The food word should only be used for training or in a true emergency situation.

3. Daisy

<u>Dog's Name:</u> Daisy
<u>Owner's Name:</u> Nicole
<u>Breed:</u> Dalmatian
<u>Age:</u> 1 year
<u>Health:</u> Daisy has no known health concerns.

<u>Owner's Description of Complaint:</u> Daisy has never had a good recall, even in puppyhood, and it is getting consistently worse. Nicole states that she walks Daisy to the dog park every day, and the routine is the same: when it's time to go, Daisy runs off and won't come near her for minutes at a time. Or if Daisy gets something from another dog that she shouldn't have, she won't come back and give it up. When Nicole wants to take Daisy to the groomer or the vet, Daisy hides in the house; Nicole has to go find her and leash her to get her in the car. Possibly worst of all, Daisy steals things in the house and then runs off and hides with them. Nicole is genuinely concerned that Daisy is going to eat something dangerous and end up sick, or run off at the dog park and get hit by a car because she won't come when called.

<u>General Temperament and Routine:</u> Daisy is loose in Nicole's small yard when Nicole is at work. When Nicole comes home, they eat dinner. Their evening culminates with a trip to the dog park in the early evening. They come home when it starts to get dark, which usually allows for about twenty minutes of exercise followed by a short walk home. On weekends Daisy fares better, and she often stays at the dog park for an hour or more while Nicole socializes with her neighbors. Daisy is much more cooperative about leaving on the weekends when they aren't so pressed for time. Sometimes Daisy even comes and sits near Nicole when it's almost time to leave.

<u>What has been attempted to solve the problem:</u> Nicole has tried trapping Daisy at the dog park, but she quickly realized that she had no chance of outrunning her dog. She also brings treats to the dog park, which helps, but it still takes several minutes for Daisy to choose to come back.

<u>Discussion:</u> There are two distinct issues here. First, Daisy just barely gets enough exercise for her breed. She needs more! Dalmatians are bred to run and move, so they benefit from significant daily exercise. Nicole is doing her best, which is why she takes her to the dog park every night after work, but the twenty minutes she spends there is simply not sufficient for a young and energetic Dalmatian. Asking Daisy to willingly come when called in order to head home after a short round of exercise is asking a lot.

The second issue is the lack of formal recall training with an emphasis on making it fun for Daisy. When Daisy is called, it is usually followed up with something unpleasant, like a trip to the vet, leaving the dog park, or having something taken away from her. Rarely is Daisy called simply to be given a free treat, petting, or praise. This is making Daisy leery of being called. In addition, calling Daisy to take things away from her is making Daisy possessive of items she finds, which can quickly lead to the dangerous habit of gulping down found objects simply to avoid losing them.

<u>Conclusion:</u> Daisy needs more exercise, and has developed a negative association with her recall cue.

<u>Solution:</u> Daisy would benefit from a few things. First, a midday run would do wonders for her overall need to move her body, making her much more likely to cooperate when it's time to leave the dog park. If Nicole can't leave work during the day, she might consider hiring a dog walker.

Second, Daisy needs to develop a new association with being asked to come. To do this, Nicole should start calling Daisy very frequently, giving her a treat, and then sending her away again. Start this at the dog park within a minute or two of arriving, and call her several times over the next twenty minutes, each time treating her and sending her back to play with her friends. Nicole should also feed Daisy dinner after her trip to the dog park; if Daisy is hungry she will be more willing to return for a treat while she is developing her new habit.

Third, place safe objects on the floor for Daisy to find. When Daisy picks the item up, Nicole should encourage her to bring it over, trade the object for a delicious treat, and then Nicole should give the object back. Keeping Daisy on leash for her early lessons will probably be helpful. Daisy needs to learn that having objects doesn't mean they will be taken away. In the future, if Daisy finds things in the house, Nicole should always trade for the object with a cookie. Indeed, if the thing is safe and there is no harm in having it, let her have it back!

The process of making recalls pleasant is not hard to do. A good rule of thumb would be four "free" recalls for every "real" recall. Never call your dog if you plan to do anything that the dog will consider unpleasant!

4. Joey

Dog's Name: Joey
Owner's Name: Donna
Breed: Standard Poodle
Age: 2 years
Health: Joey has no known health issues.

Owner's Description of Complaint: Joey generally has a reliable recall in the house; the primary issue is when he is in the back yard and Donna wants him to come in for the evening. In these instances, Joey will only come IF Donna has great food AND holds it out for him to see AND he decides he wants it. If Joey sees the food and decides it's not what he wants, he stays back 20 feet and waits to see what else might be offered. Other days he comes part way in before changing his mind and running off again. Sometimes Joey will come close, snatch the food, and then take off again before Donna has a chance grab his collar.

General Temperament and Routine: Joey is Donna's running partner, so he gets a long run every morning before she goes to work. A house sitter comes in at noon to let him out to use the bathroom. In the evening Donna plays ball will him in the yard for even more exercise. He also gets a good deal of mental exercise; Joey has a wide range of tricks

Donna has taught him that he enjoys showing off.

<u>What has been attempted to solve the problem:</u> Joey was initially trained to come with food, so he has a positive association with recalls. Donna normally shows him what food she has, or even throws a piece on the ground between them. If he wants it, he'll come the rest of the way. If he doesn't, he stays away until Donna looks for something else to entice him.

<u>Discussion:</u> Joey has a classic case of "I'll come if it's worth my while," which is one of the most frustrating situations for owners. Owners of such dogs strongly believe that the dog knows what is desired but chooses to play games rather than cooperating. The dog appears to be endlessly calculating the value of each move, leaving the owners irritated and desperate.

This recall problem is inadvertently taught by the owner early in the training process. The dog is shown what he'll get if he comes when called and is soon in the habit of making sure there is reward available AND that it meets expectations in terms of quality. This is an extremely common training error made by less experienced owners. Fortunately, it's easy to fix.

<u>Conclusion:</u> Joey understands what is desired and chooses when to cooperate.

<u>Solution:</u> Donna needs to turn Joey into an optimistic gambler who has faith that coming when called will be worth his while.

To start, Donna should get some very good food and place it where she has quick access to it, but is not on her body. Then, while in the house, Donna will call Joey. Joey has a good habit of coming on cue in the house, so odds are excellent that he will come when called. When he does, Donna and Joey will run to the food and Donna will give him several pieces. Donna should repeat this until Joey understands Donna has access to food, even if she isn't holding it in her hand or has it in her pocket. The advantage to not carrying the food on her body is that she doesn't have to pre-plan her training; she can simply go to the fridge or cabinet when she wishes to reward Joey.

If Joey does not come when called, that's fine. Donna will go and get the most delicious food item she can find. Joey will notice and come to get it! But it's too late; Donna will eat it. Herself. A few minutes later she will call Joey again. This time, odds are excellent that he will come. Donna should reward him for that choice!

When Joey's recall habit is strong in the house even when Donna has no food on her body, Donna will take this same game to the back door. Once again, Donna will call Joey, but show him nothing. If he comes, they will go get an excellent snack together. If he doesn't come, Donna will simply shut the door, leaving him outside. Donna will go get a snack for herself, return to the door, and eat it where Joey can see her doing so. If Donna has another dog, she can also choose to give the food to the other dog, making a huge production out of it so Joey knows exactly what he's missing out on. After a few minutes, Donna will call Joey again. He'll probably come, and when he does, she will make sure it is worth his while! As a side note, Donna should start this training when it doesn't matter if he comes or not.

The point of these exercises is to teach Joey that he cannot predict in advance what food might be offered to him or where that food might come from. He can come in and find out or he can stay outside and do without - and he will do without, because Donna will get a high quality snack for herself 100% of the time! The advantage to this method is that it can be applied effectively after either good or poor behavior, giving Donna the power to influence Joey after he has made his decision. If he comes, great! He gets a good snack. If he does not come, that's fine too. She will eat the good snack herself - the one he didn't realize she had access to.

Donna would also benefit from developing a pattern of "ask first and reward later" across all behaviors. For example, when she asks him to do a trick, she should keep the cookies in her pocket until the behavior is completed, then give him the cookie. If he chooses not to perform, she can take a cookie out of the fridge and eat it herself. He'll get the idea. When she wants him to go in his crate and he looks at her with a "Where's my cookie?" expression, she can ask nicely and point to his crate. Cooperation? Joey gets a cookie in his crate. No cooperation? The cookie goes in the crate, but the crate door will then be shut and locked with Joey on the outside. After a few minutes Donna can open the door, retrieve the cookie, and try again. Odds of cooperation on the second attempt are excellent.

Joey's recall will improve as a result of developing a new pattern of showing the reward AFTER the behavior takes place rather than as a bribe that is shown to Joey beforehand.

5. Kylie and Thor

<u>Dogs' Names:</u> Kylie and Thor
<u>Owner's Name:</u> Joe
<u>Breeds:</u> Alaskan Husky and German Shepherd
<u>Ages:</u> 2 years and 7 years
<u>Health:</u> Both dogs are in generally good health.

<u>Owner's Description of Complaint:</u> Joe adopted both Kylie and Thor from a local rescue group; he wanted two dogs so they could keep each other company during the day. For the most part, that works. The dogs get along extremely well and hang out together almost all the time. The problem comes when it's time to take them for walks. As soon as the leashes come off, they run off, rarely listening to Joe at all. It's almost impossible to get them to come back until they are exhausted. Joe is frustrated that the dogs seem to have no desire to stay close to him, preferring each other for company. Joe wants to train both dogs to come when called.

<u>General Temperament and Routine:</u> Joe takes both dogs for off-leash dog walks on a daily basis. Although Thor tends to stay fairly close to Joe, Kylie has a tendency to wander off. This isn't surprising since

Kylie is a Husky, a breed known for its independence, while Thor is a herding breed that tends to work with people more cooperatively.

<u>What has been attempted to solve the problem:</u> Joe praises them when they come back. He has also brought some food along on walks, but that hasn't helped much at all.

<u>Discussion:</u> The dogs appear to be very bonded to each other, but not to Joe. They have developed a habit of relying on each other rather than Joe. While it is understandable that he got two dogs so they would have company during the day, it's asking a lot for the dogs to turn to him for direction and companionship when he wants it.

Joe has not done much with the dogs one-on-one, and dogs need to be trained individually. Dog training is hard enough when the owner is concentrating on one dog; trying to pay attention to rewarding the good behavior of two dogs at once is almost impossible. And even if Joe does work with each dog alone for a period of time, a concentrated effort must be made to work with them together in low distraction environments because the dogs will fire each other up when they're together - especially on walks, where their emotions are going to take over! Trying to compete with a strong innate motivator like play with two heavily bonded dogs is doomed to fail.

<u>Conclusion:</u> The dogs are not trained to cooperate under high arousal conditions, nor do they look to Joe for direction or relationship.

<u>Solution:</u> Joe needs to start working with each dog individually. For ten minutes a day, take only one dog out. Play with that dog! Run with that dog! Feed that dog cookies! Train that dog! Every day. This alone will make a big difference in how the dogs relate to him.

After he has developed a relationship with each dog alone, he can bring both dogs out for joint training sessions, but only in low distraction environments. He should start in a small space so that the dogs do not run and play together; if they do, that will raise the intensity level so that Joe will no longer be able to compete. As the dogs show the ability to pay attention to him and whatever motivators (cookies or toys) he might have to offer, then Joe can move to more distracting environments. A typical progression might be practicing in the house, then the back yard, then the front yard.

A long line should be used for safety at first. When it's time to remove it, Joe should only let one dog go. Since Thor, the German Shepherd, seems to naturally stay closer, it would make sense to let him off leash first while keeping Husky Kylie on a leash. Joe should feed Kylie lots of cookies while Thor is loose; this will encourage Kylie to stay close to Joe. If Kylie appears frustrated and trying to get to her friend Thor, there is no way that she'll be successful off leash. When Thor shows that he can be calm and stay close when off leash, then switch and have Thor on leash and Kylie loose and repeat the procedure. When both dogs stay calm in low distraction environments, the challenge level can be increased.

On every outing with both dogs, it would be wise to call both dogs back very frequently for free cookies, then set them free again. This "checking in" will become a habit, and Joe should strongly encourage that with free cookies every time they come back on their own.

6. Tickle

<u>Dog's Name:</u> Tickle
<u>Owner's Name:</u> Chris
<u>Breed:</u> Labradoodle
<u>Age:</u> 2 years
<u>Health:</u> Tickle has mild separation anxiety but otherwise appears physically healthy.

<u>Owner's Description of Complaint:</u> Tickle is being trained in the sport of agility, which both Tickle and Chris enjoy. Unfortunately, Tickle has developed a habit of running off in the middle of agility class. Sometimes she runs to visit other dogs, while other times she just runs all over the place. Their instructor has told Chris that she cannot

continue in class if this problem is not resolved.

<u>General Temperament and Routine:</u> Tickle and Chris practice agility in the backyard everyday, which gives Tickle the exercise that she needs without taking her out in public. Before Tickle started agility training, she was a challenging young dog. She would get into everything, chew nonstop, and move constantly through the house. Tickle is a nervous dog in general. She loves to greet dogs but struggles to do so appropriately; she becomes very hyper and irritating in their presence. Before they started agility classes, Tickle and Chris used to go to the dog park, but after a few bad episodes where Tickle was chased and frightened by other dogs, Tickle refused to get out of the car when they arrived so they stopped going to the park.

<u>What has been attempted to solve the problem:</u> When Tickle runs away at class, Chris eventually catches her and puts her in a crate to teach her that running away ends the fun. This has not helped; indeed, it seems that Tickle is becoming harder and harder to catch.

<u>Discussion:</u> Tickle is showing classic signs of a stressed dog. It is common for dogs who have had bad experiences with other dogs or people to exhibit hyper-greeting behavior. These dogs appear extremely enthusiastic about greeting, but approach awkwardly out of nervousness, which others find irritating. That tends to make things worse; the dogs can't stop from approaching, yet get into trouble when they do, creating a vicious cycle.

It is also common for dogs to run when they are distressed and overwhelmed; dog sports competitors call this behavior "zooming." It is notable that when Tickle runs off at class, she usually runs around madly and with no purpose. She may run up to other dogs hysterically, but when they rebuff her, she simply continues to run and does not return to her owner. Being crated when she does return to Chris seems to be making the problem worse, likely due to her mild separation anxiety. Crating doesn't calm her down, but actually makes her feel worse!

The problem is compounded by Chris' emotions. She is also stressed! She is at risk of being kicked out of class, so she is putting even more pressure on Tickle to behave. She stays close and has a vaguely threatening tone in her voice, which often turns into hysterical yelling when Tickle runs off. The stress and pressure that Chris feels is most certainly being communicated to Tickle, who simply cannot handle the increased pressure.

<u>Conclusion:</u> Tickle has a stress problem, not a recall problem.

<u>Solution:</u> Tickle needs to get out of the habit of running off in agility class. Since this habit is due to her stress, Chris needs to remove the trigger that is upsetting Tickle - the other dogs in class. The easiest way to do this is to leave the group class and take private lessons for a period of time. This will allow Tickle and Chris to continue training in the sport they love while helping Tickle develop new habits.

Meanwhile, Tickle and Chris can continue to attend their weekly class for exposure to the other dogs - but not to work! They should set up far enough away from the other dogs that Tickle can relax while watching the other dogs. Chris should not ask Tickle for any work, but rather play with her and feed her some treats. After several weeks of this, it is very likely that Tickle will begin to relax. Chris should not reintroduce work in the class setting until Tickle is doing well in private lessons AND has demonstrated that she is calm and comfortable in the agility environment when she is not being asked to work.

Since Tickle is afraid to return to Chris because she knows that she'll be punished by being put in a crate - just like a child who is afraid to return home because he knows that he is in trouble - Chris needs to change her response when Tickle does run off. This might involve some acting, with Chris pretending that she's not upset even if she is. As Tickle's responses improve, Chris' reactions are likely to improve as well, especially if Chris understands that her dog is running out of distress, not for fun. When Tickle realizes that Chris is not angry with her, she's going to be much more likely to return quickly and on her own. And when Tickle does come back, Chris should give her a few cookies, not crate her! Chris and Tickle need to become friends again; the stress resulting from Tickle's habit of running off has seriously eroded their relationship and enthusiasm for being together.

Unlike other dogs with recall issues, keeping Tickle on leash is not the answer. Tickle does not run off and refuse to return because she's having fun; she's simply stressed, and running helps to relieve that for her. In short, she cannot do better.

7. Chloe

Dog's Name: Chloe
Owner's Name: Jeremy
Breed: Vizsla
Age: 3 years
Health: Chloe appears to be in good health.

Owner's Description of Complaint: After religiously attending three rounds of training classes with Chloe, Jeremy is terribly disappointed. He purchased Chloe as a hunting companion, and while she hunts acceptably well, she does not come when she is called. Indeed, when she is called, she does an excellent imitation of stay; she sinks to the ground and does absolutely nothing. She does not avoid Jeremy when he takes her by the collar and leads her back in, but there has been no improvement in her recall behavior at all.

General Temperament and Routine: Jeremy likes routine and structure. Each morning he wakes up early and takes Chloe for a long run. She then works on her obedience exercises for a few minutes before he goes to work. He works with Chloe on her hunting skills in the evenings, and she performs adequately but with no enthusiasm.

What has been attempted to solve the problem: Jeremy trains every day exactly the same way. To teach the recall, he called Chloe's name and then reeled her in with the leash, praising her when she arrived. He has added cookies to some of her recalls to try to make her more enthusiastic, but she refuses the food when they are working on recalls so he has stopped bothering.

Discussion: If you try a technique over a long period of time without positive results, then you need to make a change. This is particularly true if the animal is showing behaviors that might express distress. In this case, Chloe's body language shows a complete lack of physical and mental engagement, as exhibited by looking away, sinking to the ground, moving very little, and refusing food; these are all classic signs of shutting down. Refusing food is generally considered a late indicator of stress, which means something should have changed a long time ago. Chloe is not trying to do something else; she simply does not want to go back to Jeremy, suggesting there is a fundamental issue with their relationship!

Dogs with softer temperaments can be easily upset. Whereas another dog may not have even noticed being reeled in on the leash, a more sensitive dog like Chloe may take it as an enormous correction to be pulled by the collar. Even Jeremy's generic disappointment with Chloe is easily read by a sensitive dog, and dogs tend to avoid those who emanate disappointment or frustration. Jeremy and Chloe have found themselves in a bad feedback loop; he's disappointed in her reactions to training, which makes her want to avoid him. The more she wants to avoid him, the more he feel frustrated, and the circle continues. These sorts of negative feedback loops can completely poison a relationship between a dog and a person.

Solution: It's time to start over. Give Chloe a break from all training for several days. When Jeremy restarts Chloe's training, all training should be hands off; no leash and no touching her collar.

Jeremy should start with simple food tosses to get her moving. To do this, Jeremy should throw a morsel of food in one direction and let Chloe chase and eat it, then throw another piece in a new direction. He will continue with this simple game until Chloe is looking at Jeremy with her ears up and her eyes bright, at which point he can begin to encourage her to come to him for a free cookie - then back to more food tossing games! He can add in simple games of chase where he runs away; when Chloe shows up, Jeremy should give her a handful of food and then take off in a new direction.

There should be no formal cues at all during this process. When Jeremy does add a recall cue, he should change the word so there is no association with her prior training. He should also avoid all formal recalls where he faces Chloe, and instead work on informal recalls games for just a few minutes a day until she's bright and excited about her training time.

When Chloe is happy to be with Jeremy and enjoying her training, he can use less food, but he should always give her something when she shows up. Jeremy also needs to watch his tone of voice very carefully and think in terms of inviting Chloe to join him rather than commanding her to show up. Because she is not running off or showing any signs of disobedience, all of this training can take place where it is convenient; once Chloe understands what Jeremy wants and she is looking forward to complying, then he can take the behavior back out into the field where they go hunting. And if she ever fails to come? That's okay! Cheerfully encourage her and praise like crazy when she starts moving in the right direction.

Summary

I hope the case studies in this chapter have helped you understand how even specific training issues might not be what they appear to be at first glance. In this chapter, we met dogs who failed to recall due to emotional distress, excitement, innate qualities of temperament, unmet physical needs, and training choices made by the handlers. In each case, the appropriate solution required an understanding of the root problem, followed by an answer that addressed the core issues, while simultaneously making the dog enthusiastic about the recall cue.

In the next chapter we'll continue on this path, but without specific case studies. We'll look at a few more training and behavior challenges and ask ourselves how we might consider the issue at the most fundamental level.

Chapter 8
And All the Rest!

How many ways do dogs and humans live in conflict?

A lot.

Here's a rough list of things that dogs do that annoy their humans: digging, chewing, eliminating in the house, raiding the trash can, bothering the cat, fence fighting, barking at the mailman, biting, snapping or growling at people, refusing to go in a crate, being distressed in the car, stealing food off the counters, wanting to be in the house when owner wants the dog in the yard, wanting to be in the yard when owner wants the dog in house, waking up too early, being too playful, not being playful enough, whining, humping, chasing the vacuum, playing too roughly with other dogs or people, being too friendly with people, not being friendly enough with people, stealing the kids' toys, jumping up on people, eating poop, sniffing everything, dashing out the open door, rolling in dead things, stealing stuff from around the house, resource guarding, escaping from the yard, pulling on leash, and failing to come when called. For sure, there's more, but we'll stop there.

All of these things can be annoying, but behavior does not simply stop because we want it to. The fact that we're annoyed changes nothing. No more than human infants can stop crying after being stuck by a diaper pin, our dogs cannot stop barking under a wide variety of anxiety-producing circumstances. To change the behavior, you need to understand why it exists, what purpose it serves, and then determine a course of action that satisfies the underlying needs of the animal. In this chapter, we'll do just that. Let's take another look at where you might start with your core concerns about your dog's behavior.

Asking the Right Questions

Your first question should be, what is the dog's emotional state at the time the behavior occurs? Related to this, does the behavior in any way influence that emotion? Sometimes you'll need to stop the behavior in order to change the emotion. For example, let's say your dog runs madly around the house when guests come over and you want to stop that behavior. If your dog is running around the house because he's excited, the behavior of running around the house will increase his excitement. You need to stop that behavior because the activity of running through the house is exacerbating the emotion that you need to change.

At other times, you need to change the emotion before you can stop the behavior. Maybe your fearful dog growls when he is feeling trapped or uncomfortable, and you want your dog to stop growling. That growl gives you valuable information; your dog is communicating distress. If you get your dog to stop growling without changing his emotional reaction of fear, what will prevent the dog from simply biting when he's put in a situation that he cannot handle? In short, if a behavior offers a useful coping mechanism or warning for you, don't eliminate it unless you have an alternative that will serve the same purpose for the dog.

When faced with an annoying or challenging behavior, the most common emotions that you need to consider are excitement, joy, fear, anger, and boredom. In all cases, your dog needs to be in a thinking frame of mind (not too happy, or too sad, or too fearful) if you want to train your dog and change problematic behaviors.

For example, if your dog is overly excited, what behaviors might you see? He might be jumping on you or guests, running out the door, failing to stay when asked or come when called, submissively urinating, refusing to go outside, and so on. How might you address that core issue of being overly excited? You have options! Consider what purpose the behavior might serve for the dog and select an option from that point. How about dropping food on the floor to redirect his energy, or getting down on his level so he can greet you, or keeping a toy by the door to give him when you walk through the door to keep him busy, or using a calm voice and lowering your hands when you return, or training him to go to his dog bed when you walk through the door?

If your dog is scared, what might you see? Refusing to hold a stay when people approach, avoiding you when you call, submissively urinating in the house, running away and not returning when called, barking or lunging at people, refusing to come out of the crate, refusing to go outside in the dark or alone, barking, whining, howling, obsessively chewing, engaging in self-mutilation, drooling, excessive movement, or almost no movement at all. And what might you do to make your dog feel better? Remove your dog from the situation or allow him to leave on his own, giving him as much distance as he needs to relax. Quietly sit with your dog with a soothing demeanor. Give your dog an object to hold or chew. Feed your dog a snack, one small piece at a time. Give your dog a puzzle toy to work at. You have options! Always start by getting as far from the thing that is upsetting your dog as you can, and from there do what makes your dog feel better.

The more your dog experiences fear in a given context, the more easily his emotions will resort to feeling fearful, so avoid that context whenever you can! Learn to look for the triggers that cause your dog to feel fear and avoid them. At the same time, you can help your dog feel safe in the presence of those triggers by allowing your dog to decide when he is ready to approach; your job is simply to help support your dog's decisions.

Here's a human example. If you are afraid of rats and you enter a house where you have seen rats in the past, your emotions will be on high alert. If you hear a quick noise, you'll find yourself feeling fearful even before you look to see what caused it. The more times you feel fearful in that environment, the more quickly you'll feel fearful going forwards. So when it comes to the negative emotions, avoid them as much as possible!

Now let's say a good friend is willing to help you with your fear of rats. The most important thing she can do is keep you company as you explore how close you can get to the house without feeling upset. Your friend might also hold you back if you had a sudden urge to "face your fears" and run straight in. Mostly, your friend is there to support you and tell you how brave you are as you inch closer... when you are ready, but no sooner.

It's the same with your dog. Be there for support, but otherwise let your dog decide when he is ready to inch closer. The one caveat about dogs and fear: sometimes (actually, often) dogs will actively approach things that they are afraid of, possibly to get a better look at the "enemy" or to yell "back off!" - especially if the fear-inducing stimulus is a person or another dog. If you see your dog going forwards in a manner that suggests fear or discomfort, or if you've noticed your dog has gone towards things in the past, only to start barking when close, then hold your dog back and get further away. Your dog is about to make a bad decision and you want to prevent that.

If your dog is angry, what might you see? Discomfort when approached, high levels of movement and agitation, low growling with a puffed up demeanor, hard eye contact, hackles erect up the neck and back, a stiff and upright tail, or stiff movements without eye contact. And what might you do to make your dog feel better? Remove him from the situation, and don't allow him to make eye contact or get close to the things that tend to exacerbate his anger. Give him a specific alternative activity to engage in when he's in the presence of dogs that tend to upset him. As with fear, the more your dog feels anger, the faster he'll go there - so avoid those situations!

If your dog is bored, what might you see? Quite possibly digging, eating poop, getting into your trash, bothering the cat, excessive movement in the house, chewing your belongings, nudging you with his nose, howling, and so on. And how might you address that boredom? Try giving your dog more things to do: chews, toys, or more personal attention. You could also manage your dog by crating him when you cannot offer more attention.

And your dog who constantly barks at you or scratches at your leg or doors? Maybe that dog is trying to communicate with you. How about teaching him an alternative way to get your attention that you like better, like sitting quietly and staring at you, or ringing a bell when he needs to go outside.

Once you've examined the problem behavior and addressed the emotions involved, your next question should be, is there is a physical component to the problem?

If your dog is not getting enough exercise, what might happen? You may well see door dashing, jumping on people, stealing stuff to get you to play a game of chase, or pulling on a leash. And how might you address that core issue of lack of exercise? Play ball in your yard, pay a neighbor to come in and walk your dog, or arrange for doggy playdates.

If your dog is in physical pain, you'll often see issues with aggression, avoiding people, self mutilation, whining, and generally irritable behavior. Solve the underlying issue, and the behavior will be much easier to address. For example, if your dog is teething, how can you prevent your dog from chewing your woodwork? Give him plenty of other things to chew and don't leave your puppy unsupervised in your house!

If your dog is in mental pain, you might see a refusal to crate quietly, an unwillingness to go in a crate at all, whining, barking, growling at people, avoidance of the car, and more. Solve the mental pain through medication or a training plan. Remember, when working with mental disorders, you'll want to consult a veterinary behaviorist if possible.

If your dog is in a good place emotionally and you do not suspect physical or mental pain, then it's time to consider your dog's innate temperament.

What behaviors might be a direct result of your dog's breed and innate temperament? Digging, running, barking, howling, pulling, sniffing, excessive energy, too much or too little playful behavior, fence fighting, general dog aggression, alarm barking, carrying or stealing your objects, chasing prey... all of these behaviors can be strongly influenced by your dog's genetics. Just like people, dogs are born with interests! You cannot change your dog's innate temperament, but you can work with it.

Using Training to Address the Behavior
You've considered it all. You believe that you have resolved as many underlying factors as possible and you're ready to train. Now what?

Consider what you want your dog to do as opposed to what you don't want. Your dog wants to jump on guests and you want four feet on the floor. Your dog wants to pull and you want slack in the leash. Your dog wants to beg at the table and you want the dog to rest on his dog bed. In each case, identify the alternative that you would find desirable and then set up a training plan to get you there.

If you aren't sure what alternative you'd like to see, consider the strategic use of incompatible behaviors. As often as not, you can train an incompatible behavior which will eliminate the behavior that you don't want to see. For example, if your dog is trained to eat cookies off the floor when people come in, then he cannot simultaneously have his feet up on your guests. If your dog wants the cookies that you carry on walks and you offer them at your side, then your dog cannot simultaneously eat them and pull on leash. If your dog wants to bark at the front door, he cannot do so when he is carrying his beloved toy.

Go to some trouble to prevent failure while you are training. For example, if you have a problem with counter surfing, keep food off the counters as you teach your dog not to come into the kitchen when you are preparing food. If your dog fence fights, do not allow your dog outside when your neighbor's dog is out. If your dog has housebreaking accidents behind the couch, block access to that area while you work on teaching what you do want.

If all of this sounds like a lot of work, think about whether management might not be a better long term option. The fact is, training takes time and requires maintenance. It's great to have a perfectly trained dog, but you might find that you enjoy your dog better if you live with a bit of give and take rather than worrying about perfection. Maybe using a no-pull harness solves the problem of pulling on leash instantly and humanely, while also requiring no effort on your part. You might decide that it's easier to put your dog away when your elderly neighbor visits than to teach him to be calm in her presence. You might figure out that closing the dog door at night prevents excessive barking in the yard, with no additional effort on your part. Your dog wants to eat poop? He can't if you clean it up. Your dog wants to molest the cat? He can't if the cat has a variety of high hiding spots on which to rest. Your dog wants to growl at your guests? He can't if he's crated in another room.

Sometimes you'll get lucky and management alone will change the behavior because it breaks the habit. For example, young dogs who eat socks often outgrow this habit IF they are prevented from practicing the behavior. Dogs who harass your guests often calm down as a function of age IF they don't start jumping up in the first place. In the same way that most people with toddlers find it much easier to remove valuable objects from the child's reach, you might find that removing your socks from the floor is easier than removing them from your dog's jaws - or intestines! As you are deciding what matters to you, make sure that you are adequately accounting for the rights of other people. It's okay not to teach your dog a highly reliable recall in public, but it's not okay to let that dog off leash so he can run up to other people or dogs. It's okay to allow your dog to jump up on you, but it's not okay to subject your guests to that behavior. It's okay to let your dog bark, but it's not okay if you have close neighbors who find it irritating. What are your interests? What are other people's interests? What are your dog's interests? Make a plan and then train, manage, or even ignore your dog's behavior, but ensure that you're accounting for everyone's basic needs!

Summary

Is your head reeling? Is it so hard to have a dog? No, not really. If you're realistic and take the time to ferret out what you want in a dog, and how you might get from here to there, you'll likely find that it's not too much work at all. And since preventing challenges is easier than handling them after the fact, give some thought to your personal areas of interest and your dog's innate temperament, and focus on those behaviors first!

Do you really want a dog? Yeah, you just might. If you take a moment to compare the complaints we have about our dogs with our expressed appreciation for what they bring to us, I think you might find that there's no comparison! For many people, having a dog is truly one of the great joys of life. Think about how amazing it is to have a different species living right in your house with you, offering an endless supply of unconditional love. That's worth a lot. If you can focus on the incredible joy that they bring to us, maybe that roast stolen off the counter won't bother you so much after all.

In all cases, a human who wishes to influence a dog's behavior would do well to create a plan. Start with an understanding of emotions, recognize the importance of physical and mental health, respect the fact that your dog comes with an innate temperament, and develop as strong an understanding of good training as possible.

In the next part of this book, we're going to take a closer look at our plans, specifically what worked and what didn't? Where might we have gone off the rails? It's time to do some evaluation.

Notes

Part Three:
Evaluation

If you have read the first two parts of this book, then you should have a sense of your dog's basic tendencies in his emotions and temperament, and you understand the role of physical and mental health in behavior. Using this information, you not only know what problem behaviors you would like to address, but you also think you know what might be causing them. You've given serious thought to designing a training or management plan, and you're on your way!

But there's one more thing you need to know about. As you begin your training plan, you should start to see some clear indicators that you're making progress. Progress doesn't mean a steady path to resolution because that's not how behavior works; two steps forwards and one step backwards is more likely. Even so, there are still some signs you should see, and if those signs are not present, you need to do some evaluation of what you're doing, whether or not it's working, and if not, why not.

This is a critical step in training. Unfortunately, it's often overlooked, leading to a great deal of frustration when things don't go as planned. In this part of the book, we will consider the evaluation phase of your training plan.

Chapter 9
Evaluation

You had a challenge. You evaluated your options with care. You set up a training plan and you applied it diligently. What happened?

Success! Your dog is improving! Congratulations! It takes thought to come up with the right solution to a training challenge, and if your dog's behavior is improving, then you're on the right track. Good for you!

While you're gloating about your success, take a moment to observe if there might be other positive effects of your training, maybe small things that you thought were unrelated. For example, do you find your dog looking to you more often for direction? Is your dog quicker to respond to all of your requests, not just the ones that you are currently training? Is your dog more affectionate? Does your dog appear more confident in general?

The fact is, spending time with our dogs does more than affect behavior. It also affects the underlying relationship that we have with them. It reaffirms to the dog that we really are paying attention to him, and that builds his desire to be close to us. The stronger your relationship is with your dog, the easier you will find it is to build new behaviors and expectations.

But what if you weren't so lucky? What if your dog is failing to progress... or worse, regressing? This can be incredibly frustrating. You put in a lot of time and effort trying to understand the problem and you instituted your plan with a lot of thought and care! Why do our best-laid plans fail and what can we do about it? That's what this chapter is about. But before we turn our attention to outright failure, let's take a moment to consider the more subtle signs that we're on the wrong path.

Warning Signs that Failure is Imminent

Effective training almost always includes an engaged animal, so the most critical question to ask yourself when you look at your dog is this: Does your dog want to be with you right now, doing the same thing you are?

A dog who is engaged in learning will look at the handler directly, possibly with a nice wagging tail, upright ears, and bright eyes! If your dog appears "flat" during training sessions or does not look towards you with happiness, there is a problem. If your dog is looking away or seems determined to find something else to do - like sniffing random spots of nothing on the floor - then something is wrong. If he's refusing food, you need to change something.

Worst case scenario, you may notice that your dog seems to avoid you in general, not just during training. Your dog comes when commanded but otherwise stays away. He might always appear "small" and shut down, moving very little and taking little joy in your human family. If this describes your dog, strongly consider that you may have become a source of pressure and unpleasantness rather than support and enjoyment for your dog. Fixing that should become your number one priority!

But let's say it's not like that at all! Your dog loves your company, following you from room to room and bouncing with excitement at the opportunity to do some training. Yet your training is still not progressing. Why not?

Why Training Programs Fail

There are two common reasons training programs fail: either we misdiagnosed the root problem or we applied our training "fix" incorrectly.

To understand that first reason, let's go back to our case studies and consider Flip and his barking. As you recall, Flip was being crated to handle his tendency to chew inappropriately, but soon he was barking all the time! After examining all the factors, we concluded that Flip was barking out of boredom and lack of exercise, and so the recommended solution was that Flip get a whole lot more exercise.

A month has gone by. Flip's owner has hired a local teenager to come in every day to take him on a three-mile run. Flip loves this, and he comes home exhausted… but he's still barking. What went wrong?

When your solution is not generating results, it's time to take another look. Maybe the problem wasn't being caused by what you thought. In this case, maybe Flip wasn't actually bored and under exercised, so let's consider Flip again.

When David leaves the house, Flip chews on things. Bored dogs chew on things - but so do anxious dogs. Dogs who chew on things often end up in crates for long stretches of time, and both bored dogs and anxious dogs who are crated often vocalize. David tried a bark collar, which stopped the barking. Being in a crate stopped Flip from chewing on David's items, but Flip started chewing on his body. Both bored dogs and anxious dogs tend towards self-mutilation. Since we already ruled out boredom as a cause, it could be that Flip is suffering from an anxiety problem as the root issue.

Let's say David was bound and determined to ignore the possibility of anxiety - his dog is not "mentally ill" - so he decides to keep Flip in a crate with a bark collar to stop the barking AND he's added a special cone collar around his neck to prevent him from chewing on his tail. And this will work, but Flip still needs an outlet for his anxiety, so he'll probably start chewing on something he can reach, like his paws. So should David add a muzzle to prevent chewing on his feet in addition to his tail? I hope he doesn't!

If you haven't solved the root issue of anxiety, then it will express itself in some other manner. You really don't want to end up with a muzzled dog in a crate, wearing a bark collar, who shakes, drools, and lives in misery. And of course, no one sets out to do that to their dog, but it's the kind of thing that can happen when a handler is stuck on an incorrect understanding of the problem. Piling on more and more treatments will not help because they do not address the root issue.

Is it terrible that David and his trainer may have come to the wrong initial conclusion about Flip's problem? Not at all! Sometimes the only way to determine if your initial guess is correct is to test it by setting up a training plan and seeing how it goes. That is not bad or wrong, nor does it mean that you (or your trainer) were incompetent. It means that sometimes dog training is really hard! The sign of a good trainer is being willing and able to make adjustments to the plan when evidence suggests that is in order.

But there is a second possibility! Perhaps the solution is just fine, but it wasn't applied correctly. Let's say that the teen David hired comes over every day at lunch and takes Flip for a leash walk around the block instead of a long run. Did David apply the solution? Technically, yes; Flip is getting more exercise. But a leash walk around the block is not a correct application of the solution. Flip needs vigorous exercise! A thirty minute run! Twenty minutes of playing ball! Racing around with another dog!

When applying your training solution, remember to take a look at the factors of proximity, intensity, and duration (we'll discuss these in depth in just a minute). Flip needs to get enough exercise of the right type (physical or mental?), at the right time (first thing in the morning or the middle of the day?), in the right environments (backyard ball play or walking through the neighborhood on leash?). Training advice like "get your dog more exercise" needs to be tailored to the specific dog. What works for YOUR dog? While breed does matter - Flip is an adolescent Labrador Retriever, and they tend to need significant vigorous exercise - he is also an individual. Maybe he needs something different than another dog, maybe even different than one of his littermates!

Let's consider a second example of a misapplied solution in the case of Joey, the Standard Poodle. Joey has a fine recall - IF he is going to receive especially delicious cookies! His owner, Donna, was advised to start a training protocol that no longer allowed Joey to weigh the pros and cons of coming. Specifically, she would no longer show him what he was going to get for cooperation and she had been given specific consequences that she could apply if he failed to cooperate. Yet Joey STILL fails to come when called!

As we take another look, Joey does not appear to be emotionally distressed. He does not appear sick, and Donna does not call him to do unpleasant things or to punish him. Upon further questioning, Donna shares that she did make progress for a couple of weeks. Indeed, Joey was doing so well that she decided to stop using the cookies and to substitute praise instead. Unfortunately, that approach failed to take into account one basic tenet of training, namely that the dog must value what you have to offer more than the alternative or it will not function as a motivator. Since Joey would rather play in the yard than accept five seconds of praise for his loss of freedom, Joey is back to once again weighing out his options. While reducing the total number of cookies is a reasonable goal, it must be done over time. The cold turkey approach didn't cut it for Joey.

In this case, the root problem was diagnosed accurately and an appropriate training plan was set into place. The problem occurred at the execution phase; Donna did not correctly apply the plan.

Why Dogs Don't Understand Our Plans

Sometimes dog training is hard. It's the human's responsibility to create and execute a training plan that the dog can understand and follow, but often that is easier said than done! So now, let's turn our attention to better understanding some of the reasons that training plans fail in the execution phase.

The first reason is that dogs are highly contextual. They don't pick out a single thing from the environment as salient; they tend to lump it all together as a big picture. So if you've always said "sit" with a cookie held over the dog's head while leaning forward and standing in the middle of the kitchen with the refrigerator humming in the background, then all of that is part of the cue. If you change that picture even a little bit - for example, you ask your dog to sit while you're seated in a chair - odds are that your dog will fail to respond unless you've taught him that only the word "sit" is relevant and that your body position has nothing to do with it. Conversely, odds are good that if you hold your hand over your dog's head and bend forward, then your dog will sit, even if you don't say the word. Whatever you do that causes "sit" to happen should give you some idea of what your dog has been paying attention to in your training sessions, and you may quickly discover that it isn't the word at all!

Sometimes what we think we are teaching (the word "sit") is not actually what our dogs are learning (leaning over with hand in the air means put your butt down). So when guests come to the house and your dog immediately jumps up on them because they walked in through the back door instead of through the front door, it's likely that your dog didn't learn that "don't jump on guests" applies at ALL doors. No matter who opens the door. And regardless of whether the person entering is a man or a woman, young or old, familiar or new.

When your trained dog fails to do what you believe you've trained him to do, take another look. Have you shown your dog the desired behavior in a lot of contexts until he understands the piece that you care about? You need to practice "don't jump on guests" at ALL of your doors and with a variety of people! But don't worry, it will go much faster with each new behavior that you teach. Dogs are smart like that.

Our training plans can also fail if we overface our dogs. Overfacing simply means asking more than the dog has been trained to understand. You need to make sure that you've trained your dog to be successful in varying levels of intensity, duration, and proximity. Let's use the example of not pulling on a leash to explore these concepts.

You've worked hard on this behavior around your neighborhood and you're proud of your dog! He rarely pulls on a leash now, so you take him to your child's school festival. All of a sudden, your dog is pulling like crazy; it's as if he had no training at all! You need to check to be sure the intensity, duration, and proximity are appropriate for his level of training.

Intensity: How strong is the overall pull of that environment? Is your dog very curious about what's going on? Or is the reverse true? Is your dog nervous or scared in that environment? Keep in mind that your neighborhood is quiet and the school carnival is not. There is so much stimulation coming from all angles, and that stimulation will use up your dog's capacity to remember expectations, whether that stimulation creates a curious response or a fearful one. Build up intensity in less challenging environments, one step at a time. For example, take your dog to busy environments like the front of a grocery store. Then try the school yard before or after school where he will be exposed to the rush of children. Then add dog training school where he will encounter lots of dogs. And finally, the carnival where are all of these things will come together!

Duration: How long are you asking for the behavior? If your walk around the neighborhood is 30 minutes and you've been at the school carnival for three hours, your dog may have exhausted his capacity for being good. Scale back and build up duration slowly.

Proximity: How close are you to the things that are causing your dog to pull? Proximity to distractions - whether they are attractive or scary - is a huge factor in your dog's ability to cooperate. If you're five feet from another dog and your dog has never even seen another dog close up in your neighborhood, then expect pulling. Get further away from the other dogs and slowly get closer as he shows he understands he shouldn't pull on leash.

What you do next is up to you. You can train your dog to handle all of these additional factors, or you might decide that's more trouble than it's worth for the one day a year that you head to the school festival. Maybe it's easier to either put your dog in a no-pull harness or to leave him at home.

Your training might not be well-executed if you time your reinforcers poorly. Remember, a reinforcer is something that your dog wants; it's something that you give in exchange for his cooperation. Your dog doesn't pull on a leash for several minutes? He gets a cookie. He holds his down stay on his dog bed while you prepare dinner? He gets a cookie. He comes when called? He gets a cookie.

So what happens if you use your reinforcer rather poorly? For example, he doesn't pull on the leash for a minute, then pulls for a short stretch, then doesn't pull, then pulls, then doesn't pull, and then starts to pull again, and THEN you give a cookie? You might think that you're rewarding all those times he didn't pull, but odds are pretty good that he has no idea that "not pulling" has anything to do with that cookie at all.

To be effective, a reinforcer must come within a few seconds of the correct behavior if you want the dog to understand the relationship between his behavior and the cookie. So when your dog does not pull for a few seconds, he gets a cookie immediately. After a few days you notice him staying closer to your side. The same is true with calling your dog to come. If you call him at the dog park and give him a cookie when you get to the car, he probably won't associate it with coming when you called. But if you hand over that snack the second he arrives at your feet, while you're still in the park, he'll know THAT cookie was rewarding his recall. If you frequently hand over a cookie when your dog shows up, you may well find that your recalls start to be quite excellent indeed!

What else really matters when it comes to getting your dog trained? Let's wrap up this section by talking about consistency. If your dog is sometimes allowed on your bed and other times he is not, you're going to have your work cut out for you. How is he supposed to know if it's allowed or not? If your guests sometimes encourage your dog to jump up but other times they find it annoying, how will he know what you want? And if sometimes your dog is allowed to bark in the backyard but other times you're irritated and yelling, how is your dog supposed to figure it all out?

Not only does inconsistency make training progress extremely slowly, it can also be quite damaging to your dog if he has a sensitive temperament. All dogs like consistency and clear expectations, but some dogs require them. Can you imagine living with someone who sometimes yells at you when you open the refrigerator and other times smiles cheerfully? Talk about a stressful living situation!

Strive to be consistent. You can be consistently strict or consistently lax, but work towards a set of expectations that your dog can count on. This will increase your dog's confidence in you and improve his behavior overall.

One Last Look

Do you remember Daisy, the Dalmatian who doesn't come when called? Well, even with lots of good training and a careful application of the training plan, she too is still struggling! Her owner Nicole decided to take her to the vet - just in case she'd overlooked something. And as it turns out, Daisy is deaf, a rather common problem with Dalmatians. Until now, no one had ever thought to check her hearing.

This sort of misunderstanding is surprisingly common, so before you convince yourself that you've got it right with your dog and you just need to crack down a bit, maybe take one last look.

Summary

The evolution of your dog's behavior will always reflect the appropriateness of your training choices. If you're doing a good job and offering a realistic amount of time for change to occur, then your dog's behavior will improve. However, that assumes that you're accurately assessing the root issues and applying your solutions correctly. If your dog's behavior is not improving, or worse, if your dog is regressing, then you need to change something. Start by re-evaluating all of the possibilities in the first part of this book. If you still feel confident that you're on the right path but you aren't making progress, then take another look at your training technique.

Chapter 10
The Un-Problems

A behavior is a problem because a human says it is. That way of thinking leaves us with a distinctly one-sided view of dog behavior, which this book has attempted to address on various levels. When you consider all the ways dogs annoy us, it's a wonder that anyone even wants to have a dog! It's also a wonder that dogs manage to live with us at all, since at times it appears that we are bound and determined to take the dog out of the dog.

Let's take a moment to consider a completely different point of view. Not only the dog's point of view, but the bigger picture! Before we define something as a problem, we might be wise to take another look. Let's turn our attention to the "Un-Problems."

Un-problems are those things that are not appropriate targets for change, at least not at a given moment in time. After all, we are dealing with sentient beings who have rights of their own. For example, by virtue of living with you in your house, your dog will increase the overall quantity of dirt, smell, drool, and general mess in your house. While those living in your home might find this an irritation, most rational people would also recognize that it's not the dog's responsibility to change. It's simply a reality of his existence. This doesn't change the fact that it might be a problem for others living in the house, but it is not a problem that is suitable for change.

Most people understand that the dog can't simply choose not to shed or smell! How can that possibly be called a problem? Yet, those same people might hold a much harder line when the issue at hand is one of behavior, even when that behavior is tightly linked to the reality of being a dog.

Training needs to be realistic. That's why this chapter looks at the un-problems, those things our dogs do which annoy humans, and yet shouldn't be a target of change.

Immaturity

You've just acquired a new puppy! Left to their own devices, what do puppies like to do? They like to bark, play, run through the house (sometimes with muddy feet), jump on people, put things in their mouths and chew on them, eat tasty foods, explore, sniff things, dig holes in mud and sand and dirt, and a host of other things. They do these things because they are baby dogs. Fortunately we can train our dogs to show more appropriate behaviors, which has been the point of this book, but it takes time, attention, and the natural changes that result from maturity.

Puppies learn best in short bursts when they are wide awake and a little bit bored! The same is true with children. We work with our children on becoming adults in tiny bits; we mold them over time and work on specific skills like reading, writing, and doing chores as they show a readiness to learn.

Most of us recognize the need for developmental appropriateness with small children, but not necessarily for dogs. We know that trying to potty train a six-month-old infant is not likely to go well, so we manage the behavior by using diapers. And a puppy? The human needs to take responsibility for the puppy's potty training habits. A puppy cannot hold it for a long stretch of time, so be ready to get up in the middle of the night to take him out to eliminate and to supervise him closely during the day as well.

When we take our human children to school we're not too surprised if they don't want to sit down and learn for long stretches at a time. We try to work at their pace and give them plenty of play breaks. We need to do the same for our puppies. Puppies do not focus well because they are young, not because they are bad! We need to respect each puppy's learning process, even when it's slower than another puppy's. The puppy next to you in class might have amazing focus, but that's not your puppy. Your puppy needs to grow up a bit before the lessons will stick, not because there is something wrong, but because he is a unique individual who learns at a different rate than the one next to you. He's just a puppy, not a problem!

You can't simply get rid of normal puppy behavior - even if it annoys you - without risking a very shut down dog. It's really no different than parents with unrealistic expectations who force their children into behaviors that they are not ready for. Is it possible? Yes. Is it kind? No. And there are also long-term ramifications for your relationship. Specifically, you may end up with a dog (or child) who doesn't like you very much.

The vast majority of parents simply accept the fact that they'll have to hold their children's hands when they walk on busy streets, that their meals won't be too peaceful for awhile, and that their children will need to use the bathroom at inconvenient times. And while parents often experience frustration and look forward to the coming stages when life is a little easier, they recognize that it's just the nature of small children.

When you bring home a puppy, get used to the fact that you'll have to keep him on leash to keep him safe for a while. He'll need to use the bathroom at inconvenient times, and he'll get sick and disrupt your life. But there is no problem. There's simply a puppy who still has to grow into an adult dog. These behaviors will not resolve in days or weeks; it takes many months before you'll see glimmers of the adult dog your puppy will mature into.

Your decisions early on will influence how much time your puppy chooses to voluntarily spend with you. How much time he engages with you for interaction. How much he looks to you when he isn't sure what to do. In short, how much he likes you – if at all. If you choose to observe what your dog enjoys doing, and if you find ways to inject yourself into his interests, you will find that your relationship will flourish, and that, in turn, will make all of your training much easier and simpler.

Lack of Training

Your dog likes to pull on leash! He likes to jump up on you to get closer to your face! He chews on things that belong to you! Are these problems? Well, it depends. Have you taught your dog what you want him to do? If you simply yell at your dog or yank the leash whenever his pulling irritates you, then there is a problem, but it's not with your dog. It's with you. You haven't taught your dog how to behave on a leash so he will do what dogs do innately - he will pull! That's because he wants to go where his eyes and nose lead him, likely at a much faster pace than you want to go. If you want to change his behavior, don't focus on what you want to stop (the pulling), focus on what you want to start (walking nicely on a leash).

Unlike issues of immaturity, lack of training does not improve with age. As a matter of fact, time tends to make matters worse because your dog will get larger, stronger, and more set in unpleasant habits. Your dog is simply expressing his doggy nature because you have not trained the acceptable alternatives.

If you haven't made an effort to communicate to your dog what you want under a wide variety of circumstances, then you do not have a problem; you simply have an untrained dog. Make a list of behaviors that you'd like to address, and set about helping your dog understand what you would like to see!

Be patient when you're doing this. Remember that dogs learn at different rates and it's quite hard to say what is normal because it can vary so dramatically from dog to dog. It is true that some dogs can learn a new behavior in a single session, but that is not the norm. Some dogs take a good deal of time and repetition to learn. This might be frustrating, but it's also reality. Expressing your frustration towards the animal might make you feel a little better in the moment, but it won't help your relationship with your dog.

While a good training plan should begin to show some results very quickly, often within a matter of days, true mastery and understanding will take much much longer. Your dog's constant improvement should give you hope; if you're not seeing any improvement at all, check your training plan one more time! Make sure you frequently look at your dog's behavior today compared to several weeks back so that you can admire what you have accomplished!

Issues of Breed or Temperament

People often buy a dog because they like how it looks without any consideration of how that dog acts. If you thought the cutest thing about a specific puppy was watching it career around the house at top speed but you prefer to sit on the couch, you're going to have a problem. You might love your dog to bits, but you picked the wrong dog for your situation. How much and where are you willing to compromise?

Your Beagle howls. You hate howling. Who has the problem? You, or the Beagle who was bred for a hundred generations to howl? You want to do agility competitions, but you purchased a 150 pound Mastiff who shows relatively little interest in getting off the bed, let alone running and jumping at top speed. Who has the problem? The large dog who is wisely conserving his energy or you?

In the same way that a Newfoundland tends to drool, your Beagle may love to howl and your Mastiff may love to sleep. It's useful to keep in mind that you selected a breed with those tendencies. You can be irritated at your howling Beagle or disgusted at your drool-flinging

Newfoundland, or you can accept that some breeds will come with qualities that you don't like very much.

Yelling at your dog for things he can't control makes as much sense as yelling at the sidewalk when you stub your toe. Yes, you're angry that your cup of coffee just hit the floor because your dog's wagging tail knocked it down, but your dog no more turned around and intentionally swiped it with his tail than the sidewalk leaped up and smacked your toe.

You picked your dog; your dog did not pick you. There are probably some things he doesn't like much about you either, but he deals with them. It's just like with people. Try to focus on what you love about your dog, and tolerate what is likely not changeable with amused benevolence. And the next time you get a dog, think your options through a bit more carefully.

The Challenging Dogs

Dogs with aggression and fear issues are more challenging to train than "normal" dogs. Unfortunately, as often as not, no one saw it coming. Just like when a person chooses to have human children, there's a roll of the dice. You assume your child will be physically and emotionally healthy, but sometimes it doesn't turn out that way.

If your dog ends up with challenges, be aware that changing a dog's emotional states takes much longer than teaching a dog to perform a specific behavior. If you're working with a very excitable, anxious, or angry dog, settle in. It will take time to address, and your overall quality of training needs to be better than average to see results.

It also helps to find others who have similar challenges so you don't feel so alone! The internet is filled with support groups for owners of challenging dogs. Learn to embrace what goes right, to take joy in small achievements, and to accept that disappointment and frustration are normal emotions when you don't get what you expected in your dog.

The Rare Errors

Your mature, well-trained dog will make mistakes. Maybe he'll chew up an object that doesn't belong to him, or fail to come when called, or pee in your house for the first time in a year. What do you do?

Nothing. If you think it might happen again, keep a closer eye on your dog for a few days, but stuff happens. This is especially true if it was an odd incident, like if a random deer managed to end up in your suburban neighborhood and your dog chased it. The odds of another random deer showing up is not good, so don't worry about it. Now, if deer start making a point of walking down your sidewalk, you might have to institute a training plan, but you can safely dismiss rare errors.

Summary

Labeling a behavior as a problem tells us that the handler is not getting her way, but it also tells us relatively little about the best plan of action moving forward. To solve the problem, we have to know WHY the handler is not getting her way and if her expectations are realistic! Is the dog mature enough to cooperate? Has the handler given the training enough time? Are there additional challenges as a result of the dog's breed, temperament, or underlying emotional state? Is the dog physically and mentally capable of what is being asked?

The reality of living with another species means a constant flow of give and take. What is the essence of a dog and what is the essence of a human? How can we work towards having our mutual goals met so that we can live in relative harmony the vast majority of the time?

Really think about it for a moment, what an amazing thing it is to have a dog - another species! - for a friend. A companion who will be there with you, day after day, asking for little more than something to eat and a safe place to live. Another species who will remain by your side, simply because it's your habit to cooperate with each other.

Watch your dog. Note his ability to live in the moment, to appreciate what is in front of his nose, to be curious and free. I can take a walk alone, but with a dog it's shared exploration! I have all of the benefits of solitude, time to think and breathe, but none of the disadvantages of being alone. Because I am not alone.

You'll have to put some time into your friendship with your dog, but if you think about it the right way, it's not work. As with all relationships, part of the pleasure is finding ways to have everyone's needs met. Enjoy your dog's youthful silliness even as you gently mold that into your dog's maturity. Marvel at the connection you will build with little more than the natural capacity of our species to fall in love with each other.

You can pet your dog's soft fur, share a snack, or take a walk. You can work at your computer and your dog is likely to be found nearby. And when you go to bed for the night, your dog will be there. Waiting for you. In exchange for a few meals, the occasional walk, and a bit of attention, you'll have a friend. Your dog will choose you.

Printed in Great Britain
by Amazon